Young Writers

PLAYGR... ...YS

Let your creativity flow...

ode
limrick
haiku
rhyme

North West England Vol II
Edited by Jessica Woodbridge

 Young**Writers**

First published in Great Britain in 2005 by:
Young Writers
Remus House
Coltsfoot Drive
Peterborough
PE2 9JX
Telephone: 01733 890066
Website: www.youngwriters.co.uk

SB ISBN 1 84602 215 0

Foreword

Young Writers was established in 1991 and has been passionately devoted to the promotion of reading and writing in children and young adults ever since. The quest continues today. Young Writers remains as committed to the fostering of burgeoning poetic and literary talent as ever.

This year's Young Writers competition has proven as vibrant and dynamic as ever and we are delighted to present a showcase of the best poetry from across the UK. Each poem has been carefully selected from a wealth of *Playground Poets* entries before ultimately being published in this, our thirteenth primary school poetry series.

Once again, we have been supremely impressed by the overall high quality of the entries we have received. The imagination, energy and creativity which has gone into each young writer's entry made choosing the best poems a challenging and often difficult but ultimately hugely rewarding task - the general high standard of the work submitted amply vindicating this opportunity to bring their poetry to a larger appreciative audience.

We sincerely hope you are pleased with our final selection and that you will enjoy *Playground Poets North West England Vol II* for many years to come.

Contents

Radclyffe Community Primary School, Salford

St Basil's Catholic Primary School, Halton

Elliott Hamlett (11)	48
Lyle Coombes (9)	48
Jon Fox (9)	48
Adam Jackson (11)	49
Cameron Davie (9)	49
Alex Rathbone (11)	50
Andrew McGowan (10)	50
Jemma Hawkes (11)	51
Emma McKeever (10)	51
Rebecca Gill (11)	52
Lauren Maxwell (11)	52
Becky Taylor (11)	53
Lewis Baines (11)	53
Courtney Wilson (9)	54
Tanya Holleran (9)	54

St Elizabeth's Catholic Primary School, Liverpool

Rebecca Morris-Murphy (11)	54
Josh Griffiths (11)	55
Kayleigh Roach (11)	56
Megan Grant (10)	56
Amy Lahiff (11)	57
Lewis Metcalf (11)	57

St Margaret Mary's Catholic Junior School, Liverpool

Kerry Smith (8)	58
Annie Towers (8)	58
Melissa Summers (8)	59
Chloe Duffy (9)	59
Ciarán Lambert (8)	60
David Norton (9)	60
Kathleen Marmion (9)	60
John-Michael Linnell (9)	61
Antony Riley (8)	61
Paul Jackson (8)	62
John Doolan (8)	62
Siobhan Smith (7)	63
Mary Rossiter (8)	63
Georgia Ashton (8)	64
Chloe Thompson (8)	64
Paul Ruddock (7)	65

Shannon Corfield (8)	65
Amelia Gregory (7)	66
Mark Gurrell (8)	66
Jessica Lewis (7)	66
Molly Unsworth (9)	67
Laura Manning (8)	67
Jordan Tynan (7)	68
Emily Cornwall	68
Jessica Rimmer (9)	68
Jack Currie (9)	69
Chloé Manning (8)	69
Kodee Peers (8)	70
Shahnam Kazforoosh (9)	70
Adam Jackson (9)	71
Oliver Stone (8)	71
John Connor (8)	72
Hannah Ryan (8)	72
Sarah Von Bargen (7)	73
Katelyn Webb (8)	73
Georgia Hampson (9)	74
Robert Crowney (9)	74
Luke Hughes (9)	74
Amie Calvert (8)	75
Matthew Murphy (9)	75
Faye Flynn (8)	76
Sophie Mannion (8)	76
Erin Lonergan (7)	76
Holly Shipley (7)	77
Daniel Sutherland (8)	77
Emily Sutherland (8)	77
Bethany Fearon (8)	78
Jessica Dooley (9)	78
Emily Hignett (8)	79
Kate Wilson (8)	79
Morgan Challinor	79
Alex Laidaw (7)	80
Joseph Robinson (7)	80
Gabrielle Flude (8)	80
Ellie Clarke (7)	81
Lia McHale (8)	81
Ryan Cowell (8)	82
Olivia Hussey (7)	82

Joseph McLean (8)	83
Megan Jones (7)	83
Aiden Hoffman (8)	84
Joseph Rimmer (7)	84
Elizabeth Anderson (9)	85
Abigail Wright (7)	85
Megan Brady (8)	86
Chelsea Arnold	86
Lorna McMahon (8)	87
Liam Vance (8)	88
Jessica Costigan (9)	88
Chloe Russell (8)	89
Aaron Manley (8)	89
Ceiran Hall (8)	89
Joseph Fitzpatrick (8)	90

St Mary's CE Primary School, Manchester

Daniel Grayson (9)	90
Olivia Lee (9)	90
Taylor Shaw (10)	91
Emma Tommins (9)	91
Vanessa Beckles (10)	92
Katie Butler (9)	93
Katie Pollit (9)	93
Freya Holmes	94

St Michael's CE Primary School, Manchester

Lucy Haslingden (10)	94
Heather Gofton (10)	95
Bethany Trevor (10)	95
Kirstie Luu (10)	96
Shannon Brady (10)	96
Cian Bates (10)	97
Thomas Butterworth (10)	97
Rhys Nuttall (10)	98
Ben Lee (10)	98
Marcus Rowe (10)	98
Blair Bowles (9)	99
Emily Oliver (10)	99
Meghan Dunham (10)	100
Nathan Stringer (9)	100

Eben Rayworth (9)   100
Charlotte Earnshaw (10)   101
Abigail Greatrex (9)   101
Catherine Wright (9)   101
Joel Carrigan (10)   102
Iain Bird (10)   102
Michael Butt (10)   102
Dean Feather (10)   103

Victoria Hospital Paediatric School, Blackpool
Francesca Lidgley (10)   103

Wilson's Endowed CE Primary School, Carnforth
Jessica Campbell (10)   103
Joshua Forrest (10)   104
Shannon McGuire (10)   104
Amber Perryman (11)   105
Anna Galbraith (9)   106
Georgia Mackenzie (9)   106
Megan Greenwood (9)   107
Daniel Robinson (10)   107
Jack Hobbs (11)   108
Rebeka Thomas (10)   109
Louise Plowden (11)   110
Karla Fraser (11)   110
Alec Escolme (11)   111
Molly Thomas (10)   111
Janet Wightman (11)   112
Kenya Hardie (8)   112
Scott McLachlan (10)   113
Andrew Taylor (8)   113
Zara Johnston (8)   114
Sarah Galbraith (8)   114
Ryan McLachlan (8)   115
Peter Holmes (9)   115
Katy Stevenson (7)   116
Evan Forbes-Anderson (7)   116
Emma Woodend (7)   117
Sally Wightman (9)   117
Nile Wood (9)   118
Molly Warburton (9)   118

The Poems

On The Flunch Zash Pomp

(Based on 'On The Ning Nang Nong' by Spike Milligan)

On the flunch zash pomp
Where the cars go stomp!
There's a stomp, crunch, bash
Where the rhinos go zash!

On the pomp zash flunch
All the teeth go crunch!

So it's flunch zash pomp
Cars go stomp!
Stomp, crunch, bash
Rhinos go zash!
Pomp zash flunch
Teeth go crunch!
What a mad place
The flunch zash flunch zash pomp!

Tayleh Allen (7)
Broadheath Primary School, Altrincham

On The Lash Bunch Poosh

(Based on 'On The Ning Nang Nong' by Spike Milligan)

On the lash bunch poosh
Where the cars go boosh!
There's a poosh lash bunch
Where the chocolate bars go crunch!
On the poosh bunch lash
Where the horses go plash!
So it's lash bunch poosh
Cars go boosh!
Poosh lash bunch
Chocolate bars go crunch!
Poosh bunch lash
Horses go plash!
What a noisy place to belong
Is the Lash bunch lash bunch poosh!

Emma Ballan (7)
Broadheath Primary School, Altrincham

Jing Wang Tash

(Based on 'On The Ning Nang Nong' by Spike Milligan)

On the jing wang tash
Where the eggs go crash!
There's a tash jing wang
Where the hats go clang!
On the jing wang tash
Where the cakes go crash

So it's jing wang tash
Eggs go crash!
Tash jing wang
Hats go clang!
Jing wang tash
Cakes go crash!

Samantha Hughes (8)
Broadheath Primary School, Altrincham

On The Poom Cam Flick

(Based on 'On The Ning Nang Nong' by Spike Milligan)

On the poom cam flick
Where the shoes go wick!
There's a poom cam flick
Where the doors all slam!
On the flick cam poom
Where the cows go ssss oooo mm!
So it's poom cam flick, shoes go wick!
Flick poom cam, doors all slam!
Flick cam poom, cows go ssss oooo mm!
What a noisy place to belong
Is the poom cam poom cam flick!

Jack Elliott (8)
Broadheath Primary School, Altrincham

On The Prip Snick Sap

(Based on 'On The Ning Nang Nong' by Spike Milligan)

On the prip snick sap
Where the cars go clap!
There's a sap prip snick
Where the soap goes lick!
On the sap snick prip
Where the mice go snip!
So it's prip snick sap
Cars go clap!
Sap prip snick sap
Soap goes lick!
Sap snick prip
Mice go snip!

Adam Kitchen (8)
Broadheath Primary School, Altrincham

On The Ling, Ying, Pring

(Based on 'On The Ning Nang Nong' by Spike Milligan)

On the ling, ying, pring
Where the dogs go ding!
There's a pring, ling, ying
Where the cats go wing!
On the pring, ying, ling
Where the cows go cling!
So it's ling, ying, pring
Dogs go ding!
Pring, ling, ying
Cats go wing!
Pring, ying, ling
Cows go cling!
What a noisy place to belong
Is the ling, ying, ling, ying, pring!

Chelsea Thomas (7)
Broadheath Primary School, Altrincham

On The Yump, Lash, Funch

(Based on 'On The Ning Nang Nong' by Spike Milligan)

On the yump, lash, funch
The cats go crunch!
And the pans go jibber jabber joo!
There's a lash, funch, yump
All the fish go bump!
And all the chips shout, 'Boo!'
On the funch, yump, lash
All the books go smash!
And the mice all have a clue
So it's yump, lash, funch
Cats go crunch
Lash, funch, yump
Fish go bump!
Yump, funch, lash
Books go smash!
What a noisy place to belong
Is the yump, lash, yump, lash, funch!

Emily Douthwaite (7)
Broadheath Primary School, Altrincham

On The Moosh Pick Ping

(Based on 'On The Ning Nang Nong' by Spike Milligan)

On the moosh pick ping
Where the birds go twing!
There's a ping moosh pick
Where the monkeys go click!
On the ping pick moosh
All the rocks go whoosh!

Ellie McCormick (7)
Broadheath Primary School, Altrincham

On The Lash Twick Bunch

(Based on 'On The Ning Nang Nong' by Spike Milligan)

On the lash, twick, bunch,
Where the soap goes crunch!
And the flowers la la la!
There's a bunch, lash, twick,
Where the chips go flick!
And the curtains swish, waa waa!
On the bunch, twick, lash,
All the crisps go crash!
And the teachers go bla blu bla!
So it's lash, twick, bunch
Soap goes crunch!
Bunch, lash, twick,
Chips go flick!
Bunch, twick, lash,
Crisps go crash!
What a tasty place to belong
Is the lash, twick, lash, twick, bunch!

Lakeiya Hall (8)
Broadheath Primary School, Altrincham

On The Wang Cleam Hisper

(Based on 'On The Ning Nang Nong' by Spike Milligan)

On the wang cleam hisper
Where the dogs go whisper
There's a hisper wang clam
Where the hats go scream
On the hisper wang cleam
Where the cows go bang!

Hannah Munro (8)
Broadheath Primary School, Altrincham

On The Sming Ping Scoo

(Based on 'On The Ning Nang Nong' by Spike Milligan)

On the sming ping scoo
All the mice moo!
And the monkeys jibber jabber joo!
There's a scoo sming ping
Where the parrots all sing!
And the church bells ring, ring, ring!
On the scoo ping sming
Where the eggs go ting!
And you just can't eat them when they do
So it's sming ping scoo
Mice go moo!
Scoo sming ping parrots all sing!
Scoo ping sming
Eggs go ting!
What a noisy place to belong
Is the sming ping sming ping scoo!

Ben Fitton (8)
Broadheath Primary School, Altrincham

On The Pick Tuzz Boar

(Based on 'On The Ning Nang Nong' by Spike Milligan)

On the pick tuzz boar
Where the lions go roar
There's a boar pick tuzz
Where the monkeys go buzz
On the boar tuzz pick
All the bears go tick.

Dylan Nazarowicz (8)
Broadheath Primary School, Altrincham

On The Zing, Tick, Nash

(Based on 'On The Ning Nang Nong' by Spike Milligan)

On the zing, tick, nash
All the puppies go smash!
There's a nash, zing, tick
All the mice go flick!
On the nash, tick, zing
All the dogs go ding!
And the chickens go smash!
So it's zing, tick, nash
Puppies go smash, nash, zing, tick
Mice go flick!
Nash, tick, zing
Dogs go ping
What a noisy place to belong
Is the zing, tick, zing, tick, nash!

Leah Williams (8)
Broadheath Primary School, Altrincham

On The Jing Pang Tang

(Based on 'On The Ning Nang Nong' by Spike Milligan)

On the jing pang tang
Where the eggs go plang!
There's a tang jing pang
Where the cakes go clang!
On the tang pang jing
Where the hats go ping!
So it's jing pang tang
Eggs go plang
Tang jing pang
Cakes go clang
Tang pang jing
Hats go ping
What a noisy place to belong
Is the jing pang tang!

Lauren Shepherd (8)
Broadheath Primary School, Altrincham

On The Fash, Ling, Pring

(Based on 'On The Ning Nang Nong' by Spike Milligan)

On the fash, ling, pring
Where the cats go ring!
There's a pring, fash, ling,
Where the people go ting!
On the pring, ling, fash,
Where the keys go bash!
So it's fash, ling, pring,
Cats go ring,
Pring, fash, ling,
People go ting!
Pring, ling, fash,
Keys go bash!
What a noisy place to belong
Is the fash, ling, fash, ling, pring!

Elisha Grizzle (8)
Broadheath Primary School, Altrincham

On The Toosh Cleet Tunch

(Based on 'On The Ning Nang Nong' by Spike Milligan)

On the toosh, cleet, tunch
Where the horses go crunch!
There's a funch, toosh, cleet,
Where the sheep go bleet!
On the tunch, cleet, toosh,
Where the eggs go whoosh!
So it's toosh, cleet, funch,
Horses go crunch!
Tunch, toosh, cleet,
Sheep go bleet!
Tunch, cleet, toosh,
Eggs go whoosh!
What a scary place to belong
Is the toosh, cleet, toosh, cleet, funch!

Georgia Spencer (7)
Broadheath Primary School, Altrincham

On The Posh Pomp Swing

(Based on 'On The Ning Nang Nong' by Spike Milligan)

On the pash pomp swing
Where the monkeys go ping
There's a swing pash pomp
Where the hats go stomp
On the pash pomp swing
All the cakes go ping.

Callum Hughes (7)
Broadheath Primary School, Altrincham

The Best Diva *Ever!*

The best diva ever is really cool and funny
The best diva ever has loads of money
She's always giving me sweets
And lots and lots of treats
And yes, she's the best diva ever

The best diva ever has short brown hair
She's always there when I need the care
She has twinkling blue eyes
Always giving me a surprise
And you know what? She's the best diva ever

The best diva ever cheers me up when I'm down
She makes me smile when I've got a frown
She picks me up when I'm sore
Although her favourite animal's a wild *boar!*
Yes, you guessed it, she's the best diva ever.

You still haven't guessed who it is?
Wow, I can't believe it!
Come on, it's easy
I'm gonna burst
Say it
My mum is the best diva ever!

Kathy Stones (10)
Catforth Primary School, Preston

Faster Fudge

I go to school with Fudge
He often doesn't budge
He lies around in his cage

At break I shout, 'Let's go and play!'
But Fudge doesn't have a lot to say
He looks at me to pick him up
And I cuddle him like a big fat pup

Outside we play in the grass
And I can tell Fudge says,
'At last I'm free, I'm free!'
For as you can see
Fudge isn't like you and me
He's a guinea pig.

Ryan Blundell (10)
Catforth Primary School, Preston

Monsters

My toy box started rattling
My TV sprouted arms and legs
My mum started moaning
My bed got really hairy and scary
My mind started swirling and twirling
My head started whirling and whirling
My lamp jumped up and down
My mind went round and round
My mind can't take all this
My mouth can't either
My feet started dancing
My mind couldn't understand
My mum, my dad, my teacher too
Why me? Why me?
Why go for me?
The monsters have come to town!

Alexandra Butcher (10)
Catforth Primary School, Preston

I Hate Bullies!

I hate bullies, they make me mad,
They think they're really hard but they're really sad.
They go round school acting really cool, but I think they're cruel.
They all go round in a big gang, but with them I don't want to hang.
They hang round in the centre of town and they always hold me down.
They hang round in the swimming pool because they think they rule.
They pick on kids that don't fit in when all they're fit for is the bin.
I've told you once and I'm not going to tell you again
I hate bullies, they make me mad!

Oliver Whalley (10)
Catforth Primary School, Preston

Short Or *L-O-N-G*

I really don't know the attraction
Of addition and subtraction,
I've never really been that good
At doing maths like you should,
But it doesn't really matter,
After all, it's only chatter,
I don't need skills or to be clever,
Laughing is my best subject ever.

Shape and distances,
Short or l-o-n-g,
I'm always worried I'll get it wrong.

Times and division, hard to get the vision,
When you're stuck in a classroom,
It's just labour and doom.

Graphs and charts are hard to start,
I think maths is truly an art!

Nicola Birch (9)
Catforth Primary School, Preston

Computer Genius

I am a computer genius
I love it when I am serious
Isn't it quite obvious
I am delirious
My brother is fierce

I am a computer genius
I just love PC
Can't it be me?
Please, can't it be me?
I am coming to tea
Can't it be me?

I am a computer genius
Can't it be me?

Thomas McAlister (9)
Catforth Primary School, Preston

Magic Maths

Let's begin to learn to count,
We'll take you to any amount.
The numbers can be big or small,
Come on now, let's learn them all!

Counting can go up or down,
Please don't frown.
1, 2, 3, 4 and 5,
Come on class, let's feel alive!

You can have a happy face,
When you learn this simple phrase.
1, 2, 3 and 4, 5, 6, 7 and 8,
From this rhyme you will learn maths is a lesson you won't hate!

Amy Blundell (8)
Catforth Primary School, Preston

Addictions (The Strange Types)

I have some odd obsessions
You know - some really awful addictions
When I clothes shop in Preston Town, I buy from 'Attractions'
My brother says I'm full of emotion
Not likely - my mum calls me destruction

I dream of a tall black stallion
Not Spanish, no! Arabian
Because half of me is pure Italian
I want chocolates straight from Belgium
Delivered by Delta Goodrum

I have this other addiction
I always have to use alliteration
I guess it's an action
That's absolutely
Absurd!

I know all my obsessions
Are other people's creations
Gone through magnification
To make an around the world sensation
Without them I'd have a serious reaction

So somebody please have a solution
A spell or a potion
A hint or a suggestion
To point me in the right direction
Please! I've forgotten the question!

Gabriella Giannoccaro (11)
Catforth Primary School, Preston

Macavity

Macavity, Macavity, there's no one like Macavity
He likes to be in the laboratory
Once or twice he has broken his paw
There is no one like Macavity

Macavity, Macavity, there is no one with more cavities
Some people say his teeth are gold
Others say he is bold
You think you see him on the street
Then you tell the copper then another crime unfolds
Macavity's not there

Macavity, Macavity, he wrecked the Queen's tapestry
But when the Royal Guards are called
Macavity's not there

Macavity, Macavity, he is a catastrophe
He flushed Her Majesty down the lavatory
And when they found Her Majesty
Macavity wasn't there.

Fraser Mitchell (11)
Catforth Primary School, Preston

Jealousy

Jealousy is like soft, quiet, clear air destroyed by a storm.
Jealousy looks like a grey hooded person.
Jealousy reminds me of an unshared Easter egg.
Jealousy is as black as night.

Daniel Wheildon (9)
High Bentham Community Primary School, Lancaster

Anger

Anger is like fire
Sounds like people screaming
Tastes like a crunchy burnt marshmallow
Looks like a chewed pen
Feels like orange peel
Reminds me of a rotten peel.

Annie Neill (8)
High Bentham Community Primary School, Lancaster

Excitement

When I opened my eyes
I had a big surprise to see
What I could see - *all the rides!*
Do you know where I was at?
I was on the sewer rat
At Light Water Valley!

Amie Calvert (9)
High Bentham Community Primary School, Lancaster

In The Future

Will there be fresh air to breathe? What will be left?
Will plants be green? Will grass be sweet?
Will health be a word that means something?
Will fumes cover the sweet green fields?
Will fumes go through the dusty air?
Will I choke and cough when I go anywhere?
Will animals die and be extinct?
What will happen to me?

Miriam Hymer (8)
High Bentham Community Primary School, Lancaster

Anger And Hate

Anger surges through the body,
Burning every limb.
Hate boils every muscle,
Temples start to throb.
Anger is hot and red,
It sounds like a crackling fire in your brain,
It smells like burnt smoke,
It tastes like bitter salt.

Tom Parkinson (8)
High Bentham Community Primary School, Lancaster

Hope

Hope is white like polar bear's fur,
It sounds like a whistling bird,
It looks like a juicy lemon on your plate
And it smells like rhubarb crumble,
It tastes sour and sugary,
It feels like the hot sun burning on my hand,
It reminds me of pancake day.

Simon Morphet (8)
High Bentham Community Primary School, Lancaster

Anger

Anger is red
It sounds like wind blowing in my face,
It tastes like bitter water,
It smells rotten,
It feels like hot burning coals,
It reminds me of arguing.

Ayrton Harrison (9)
High Bentham Community Primary School, Lancaster

Anger!

Anger strikes up to the top,
It runs up so impatiently . . .
It feels so hot, like a volcano's top,
It's red and hot,
The taste is so bitter and plain
And it digs into your skin.

Emily Hunter (8)
High Bentham Community Primary School, Lancaster

Anger

Anger's colour is dark red
It sounds like ten volcanoes exploding
It tastes like burning chilli
It smells like burning fire
It looks like red smoke
It feels very slimy
It reminds me of poison.

Matthew Dominic Dawson (8)
High Bentham Community Primary School, Lancaster

Splendid Love

Love sounds peaceful and quiet,
It tastes of sugar and magical sweets.
The colour of love is cream and white,
Love smells of cake, chocolate and sweet.
Love looks like rosebuds blooming,
It feels like rose petals and the softest fur,
Love reminds me of my loving family!

Tina Sawyer (9)
High Bentham Community Primary School, Lancaster

Anger

Anger is like flaming hot fire,
Anger smells like burnt food,
Anger tastes like fire.
Anger looks like flames of fire,
Anger feels like there's nobody there.
The colour of anger is red.
It reminds me of when I had a fight with my brother.

Laura Semple (8)
High Bentham Community Primary School, Lancaster

Hope

Hope is the most beautiful thing in the world
The colour is like a crystal blue sea
It sounds like a person laughing
It tastes like Sunday dinner
It looks like a garden on a bright and sunny day
It feels like soft cotton wool.

Tristan Ward (8)
High Bentham Community Primary School, Lancaster

Anger

Anger is as red as lava,
It tastes like bitter salt,
It sounds like a bomb exploding,
It looks like a bad dream in my head,
It reminds me of falling out with my sister.

Evan Sutton (9)
High Bentham Community Primary School, Lancaster

I Can Hear . . .

I can hear the swish of my hair,
I can hear the lights buzzing,
I can hear the scratch of a pencil.

I can hear the clock to tick-tock,
I can hear children whisper,
I can hear a child have a drink.

I can hear the birds sing a nice song,
I can hear the tap dripping,
I can hear a child turn a page of a book.

I can hear the shutting of a door,
I can hear the wind blow,
I can hear the opening of a clip.

I can hear the opening of a gate,
I can hear a child sharpen a pencil,
I can hear a child drop a ruler.

Zara Wynne (8)
High Bentham Community Primary School, Lancaster

Embarrassed

Embarrassed is bright red,
It sounds like my heart beating fast,
It tastes like Coke gone down the wrong way,
It smells like a mistake,
It reminds me of forgetting my lines.

Katie Hannigan (9)
High Bentham Community Primary School, Lancaster

Hate

Hate is the most horrible
Emotion you've ever seen.

Hate is the most upsetting
Emotion that worries my mate.

Hate has the most horrible colour,
It is black and grey.

Hate is the most upsetting emotion
That makes me late for school.

Hate has the most awful sounds,
It sounds like funeral music.

Hate tastes like bitter salt
Out of the sea.

Hate smells like rotten eggs.

Hate feels like a warm blazing fire
That burns me to bits.

Hate reminds me of falling out
With my mate.

Harriet Whitaker (9)
High Bentham Community Primary School, Lancaster

Jealousy

Jealousy is see through
Jealousy sounds like someone screaming
Jealousy tastes like sherbet
Jealousy smells like smoke in the sky
Jealousy is not something I long to have.

Connor Elsdon (8)
High Bentham Community Primary School, Lancaster

Out Of My Window

Out of my window I can hear barking dogs,
Out of my window I can see splashing frogs.

Out of my window I can smell my delicious sweets,
Out of my window I can smell a tea treat.

Out of my window I can see raindrops
Making patterns on the windowpane.

Out of my window I can see people
Walking down the lane.

Out of my window I can almost
Feel the wind on my skin.

Out of my window I can't even
Hear the drop of a pin.

Erin Cochrane (9)
High Bentham Community Primary School, Lancaster

My Dog, Stitch

My dog, Stitch is like a witch,
He had a puppy and it was a bitch.
Stitch has got gnashing teeth
And his best mate is called Keith.

His puppy is called Sandy
And she plays with Mandy.
Sandy is always skipping with joy
And one of her mates is a boy.

Stitch is black and white
And he never pulls his collar too tight.
He goes mad over confetti
And he believes in the yeti!

Nathan Quinn (8)
Radclyffe Community Primary School, Salford

My Family Is Busy

My mum is always busy.
She's always cleaning up.
She's cleaning the pots,
Even to wash the very last cup.

My sister is always busy,
She's always going to school.
I know she thinks she's so cool,
But she's just a total fool.

We're going on a family outing,
My sister is shouting.
Her exams are mounting.
She got wet in the fountain,
Ha! Ha!

My dad is always busy,
He's going here, there
And everywhere,
But I don't care.

Crystal Williams (8)
Radclyffe Community Primary School, Salford

A Poem About My Baby Sister

My baby sister walks
On tiles for 400 miles

My baby sister cries
When she sees my mum's eyes

My baby sister moans
And groans all day long.

Jodie Carr (8)
Radclyffe Community Primary School, Salford

The Dragon Who Ate My School

The dragon's gnashing teeth
Scares the school away.
The school comes to life
In the middle of the night
And the dragon wants a fight.

The children run wild.
The dragon acts like a fool.
He blows down a house,
So the children shout like a mouse.

The dragon's scales are as sharp as a knife.
They spin through the air
And stab through the principal's hair.
The dragon flies through the air.

Jake Artus (8)
Radclyffe Community Primary School, Salford

My Sister Drives Me Crazy

My sister drives me crazy
As she runs, screams and shouts.
She's always coming after me
To try and give me a clout.

When she's in the garden
Sitting in the sun,
I turn on the water hose
And then I start to run.

My mum gets fed up
Because we always trick each other.
I wish instead of a sister
I had a brother.

Kelsey Wilson (8)
Radclyffe Community Primary School, Salford

My Journey

On Monday I
Went upstairs to
Pack my bags.

On Tuesday I
Told my dad to hurry
And then his nose
Was runny!

On Wednesday I
Got in the car,
The journey was long
And it took lots of hours.

On Thursday I
Went on the rides,
They had about eight sides.

On Friday I
Hooked a duck
And won a fish.
I went home,
I put him in a dish.

On Saturday I
Ate a chip
And had a dip.
When it was time to go,
I made a coat out of indigo.

Last of all, Sunday,
That's when I
Went swimming
And had a dip.

Tonicha Ainsworth (8)
Radclyffe Community Primary School, Salford

My Wonderful Mum And Dad

My wonderful dad is always there
To lend me a hand when I feel scared.
Along comes my mum with love and care
And whenever I need her, she's always there.

Rianne Desouza (8)
Radclyffe Community Primary School, Salford

I Can Hear

I can hear
A ladybird jumping from
Leaf to leaf,
Like the sun rising.

I can hear
A pen laughing
In my face,
Like a hip-hop hen.

I can hear a sound
Of a wolf howling
Like a T-rex,
A roaring of madness.

I can hear
The moon saying
Goodnight,
As sweet as a butterfly.

I can hear
A rocket ship
Going faster than
The speed of sound.

All I can hear is
Homer going . . .
D'oh!
Like a repeating pattern.

Nathan Modlinsky (9)
Radclyffe Community Primary School, Salford

Pets

Pets are my favourite.
Pets are funny.
Pets are wonderful.
Pets are clean.
Pets are a bit dirty.
Pets are messy.
Pets are tiny.
Pets go to sleep.
Pets are immense.
Pets are my favourite animals.
Pets are merry.
Pets are quiet.

Melissa Heenan (9)
Radclyffe Community Primary School, Salford

Spike *xxx*

My pet gerbil, Spike,
Popped my bike.

He was dead
And I found him in his bed.

Spike was eighty
And was my matey.

He liked fruit,
He crawled into my boot.

He was sweet and kind
And he didn't mind.

He was like a bun,
His eyes were as red as a burning sun.

Heather Seddon (9)
Radclyffe Community Primary School, Salford

Pets Have Gone Crazy

I see a busy bee
Taking care of his flea.

I see a pet
Going down to the vet.

I see a pony
Going loony.
(His name must be Rooney).

What's that over there?
It must be an octopus on a fair.

Ellis Foster (9)
Radclyffe Community Primary School, Salford

Falcons

Falcons fly all over the place,
The look on their face will scare you
And their jaws and their claws will attack.

Joel Davies (6)
Radclyffe Community Primary School, Salford

Watch Out!

Watch out for Codie!
Watch out for her!
She is the one
Who eats boys and girls.
If you go to her cave,
You'd better be afraid,
Because she loves kids for her tea!

Sophie Roberts (9)
Radclyffe Community Primary School, Salford

Football - Haiku

Brilliant ball play!
Kick the ball into the goal!
Go team! Go team! . . . *Goal!*

Rebecca Sharp (9), Robyn Weston & Sara Heddi (10)
Radclyffe Community Primary School, Salford

Storm

The storm is coming, roaring like a lion!
The wind is as powerful as stampeding elephants.
The clouds are as black as a jaguar.
The storm is here, scratching on the windows.

The wind is as strong as a rhino.
The thunder is as fast as a cheetah.
The storm is calming down.
It is calm like a rabbit.
The clouds are fading away.

Now it has gone.

Kyle Dempsey (10)
Radclyffe Community Primary School, Salford

My Greece Poem

The scorching sun shines so bright,
It's brighter than a starry night.
The beaches are so natural,
It's hard to believe,
The seas are so pure with breathtaking waves.
The colossal buildings high in the sky,
You can see the birds flying so high.

Melody Quincey & Ashly Walsh (10)
Radclyffe Community Primary School, Salford

Animals

Some animals are fast,
Some animals are slow.
Some animals are kind,
Some animals are fierce.
Some animals live underwater,
Some animals live on land and
Some live on both.

Devaun Miller (7)
Radclyffe Community Primary School, Salford

I Saw

I opened the door
And saw the floor
And on the floor I saw a tour
And on the tour I saw the shore.

Billy Quincey (5)
Radclyffe Community Primary School, Salford

Mums

Mums, mums, chat, chat, chat
Never stop wearing a pink hat

Mums, mums, chat, chat, chat
Always shouting at the cat

Mums, mums, chat, chat, chat
How about that?

Grant Carr (9)
Radclyffe Community Primary School, Salford

Robot

As my robot galumphs,
Its gigantic feet go *boom! boom!*

He often repeats, 'Meep, meep'
Immensely.

Crunch! Crunch!
My robot crushes everything
In its path,
With plenty of controlled
Destruction.

Hmpht, hmpht,
My robot seems to be
Slowing down.

'Meep, m..e..e..p, m....e....e....p.'
Now I have ended.

David Travis (11)
Radclyffe Community Primary School, Salford

Sunshine Greece

It is sunny in Greece,
That's why it is full of peace.

Everywhere is the sun,
That's why Greece is so much fun.

There are mountains everywhere,
That's why people stop and stare.

Night-time's begun,
That's why there's no sun.

Now it's time for bed,
So rest your weary head.

Wait for morning to come
And there will be more sun.

Gabrielle Reilly (9) & Santana Stewart (10)
Radclyffe Community Primary School, Salford

Come To Greece

The luxurious beaches full
Of tranquillity.
The islands send you into a
Dreamy imagination.
The peaceful and calm
Villas, apartments and hotels
Just make you want to stay
There forever.

In the pools you float
With your dreams
And look up into the blue sky.
The Acropolis home to the Olympics,
The palm trees swift in the breeze,
Now I bet you're dreaming of you
Next holiday in Greece!

Aimee Lomas & Lorna Benson (11)
Radclyffe Community Primary School, Salford

Greece

I am Greece.
The almighty Greece.
My ruined temples may be wrecked but leave many memories.
My sparkling white waves glitter in the sun.
My mountains are as strong as steel.

However, I will still have my wide, colossal cracks.

Maybe in a few years, I might not be here
But there will always be a faint memory of me in your mind.
But if you knew me while I was here,
You'd have so many memories already.

Leah Grech (10) & Liam Evans (9)
Radclyffe Community Primary School, Salford

Greece Poem

Greece is the greatest.
It's full of peace and quiet.
The waves are clear as air.
The sand is soft.
The sun is scorching, whilst the sea is sweet.

Karl Kirk-Childs & Cade Larkin (10)
Radclyffe Community Primary School, Salford

Haiku Poem

What? Haiku poems?
I have never heard of them!
Huh? I've just made one!

James Lowther (11) & Ashley Watson (10)
Radclyffe Community Primary School, Salford

Football - Haiku

Superb midfielder
He's a wondrous player
Chelsea fans go mad!

Ellis Parkes, Kayden Thelwell & Alex Bell (10)
Radclyffe Community Primary School, Salford

Football - Haiku

The wonderful team
Champions League, come on now!
The crowd cheers us on.

Francis McAnulty (9)
Radclyffe Community Primary School, Salford

The Litter Bug

I am a litter bug,
I live inside the bin.
I throw mostly a bit of tin.
I'll put litter in your street
With my fin.

Don't dare put litter in the bin
Or I will follow you home.
Your bed will be full of litter,
If you touch it, your hand will
Taste like butter.

You will become ill,
If you don't stay still.
Your hands will be on fire,
Then turn into wire.

Aw . . . I love a happy ending,
Oooo . . . chocolate.
Awww!

Kane Harris (9)
Radclyffe Community Primary School, Salford

My Greece Poem

My sun is brighter than Heaven,
My air is as pure as gold,
My waves slide, side by side.

My mountains are so towering,
That you cannot see them.
My people are so generous
On my little island.

Thomas Benson & Abigail Thompson (11)
Radclyffe Community Primary School, Salford

A Season Poem

Spring makes the flowers grow,
Summer makes it all aglow.
Autumn makes the leaves fall off trees
And winter, you can make a snowman.

January is really chilly,
February is fun.
March is the springtime,
April is too.

May makes flowers grow,
June is the summertime.
July, you can fly a kite,
August is really warm.

September, you can pick an apple,
October you can eat it all up.
November you can go in a hot air balloon,
December is the start of winter.

Nadjla Bougherira (10)
Radclyffe Community Primary School, Salford

I Know A Wizard's Garden

I know a wizard's garden
Where whispering breezes blow,
Where silverfish swim in a pond
And moonshine flowers grow.

I know a wizard's garden
Where bluebirds come and go,
Where golden plums hang from the bough
And sometimes there is snow.

I know a wizard's garden
Where cockerels strut and crow,
Where chocolate cats snooze in the shade
And singing streamlets flow.

Bradley Gleave (9)
Radclyffe Community Primary School, Salford

The Island Of Greece

The magnificent buildings that you can view,
The vast beaches that are so peaceful,
The colossal mountains you can explore.

The churches are known for their blue domed peaks.
The country is known for its warmth and beauty.
The views are well known to be very scenic
And they are amazing, extraordinary views!

Crickets singing you to sleep,
Waking up to a scorching sun.
There are so many beautiful thoughts to think
About Greece!

Ryan Pinkney (10) & Thomas Smith (11)
Radclyffe Community Primary School, Salford

Robot Junk

The robots go crash
The robots go bang
The robots go side to side
But all I can see
Is them looking at me
With their wobbly eyes.

Niall Cooper (10)
Radclyffe Community Primary School, Salford

My Teacher

My teacher is the best,
Better than all the rest.
I love her.
She is the best.

Rianna Barratt (7)
Radclyffe Community Primary School, Salford

School Bully

After he follows me,
Chasing me down the street,
I am racing and I fall flat
On my face.

I get back up. Run!
Suddenly he pulls out
His bb gun and he
Grabs my watch
And pulls it off.
He puts it in his pocket,
Then I run off.

At playtime he watches
At the corner of his eye.
Every time he calls me names
I start to cry.

I am sitting at my desk.
He thinks he is the best.
He throws paper at me
And I keep it and
Throw it back.

When he is getting ready
For PE, he is calling me weak.
He is talking around the corner
And I have a little peek.

Amy Dickerson (8)
Radclyffe Community Primary School, Salford

Bacon

Bacon in a pan.
Wibble wobble,
Bacon in a pan.
Go bacon!
I love you.
Sizzle.

Syrus McLoughlin (7)
Radclyffe Community Primary School, Salford

Football - Haiku

England's the best team!
The greatest player's Lampard.
He strikes like thunder!

Lewis Reilly, Theo Warmington (10) & Gabrielle Reilly (9)
Radclyffe Community Primary School, Salford

Number One

Number one, tickle my tum
Number two, I love you
Number three, come to me
Number four, run under the door
Number five, come alive.

Brooke Bellingham (6)
Radclyffe Community Primary School, Salford

Number One

Number one, touch your thumb
Number two, go to the loo
Number three, go for me
Number four, go for a snore
Number five, learn to drive.

Demi Bellingham (6)
Radclyffe Community Primary School, Salford

Moody

Moody, moody, moody me,
Moody, moody, moody she,
Moody, moody, moody he,
I'm so moody, I need a cup of tea.

Kimberley Lever (9)
Radclyffe Community Primary School, Salford

My Greece Poem

Down by the sea it is all peaceful
And cheerful.
The mountains are
Towering
And the temples are full of
Cracks.

Natasha O'Connor & Rebecca Stephenson (10)
Radclyffe Community Primary School, Salford

Greece

The scorching sun rising over the sea
And the beach waiting there for
You and me.
The scenery is great
And the mountains await.
The mountains are high,
Right up to the sky!

Zack Murray (9), Rhiannon MacDonald (11)
& Phoebe Stewart (10)
Radclyffe Community Primary School, Salford

Wiggly

Spaghetti is wiggly,
Sausages are so sizzly,
Cream crackers are so crackly and delicious,
Pancakes are so yummy, I can eat them,
Noodles are so wiggly, they are so funny,
Burgers are so hot, I hardly touch them,
Bacon is so chewy, bacon is so yummy.

Holly Quincey (7)
Radclyffe Community Primary School, Salford

All About My Baby Sister

My baby sister cries
At night
When she has
A fright
When she has no light

My baby sister
Loves my pet
And she always makes
It sweat

My baby sister
Always wakes me up
In the morning
And makes me
Breakfast.

Shannon Hillyard (8)
Radclyffe Community Primary School, Salford

Sun, Sea And Greece

The sun, the sea, the food.
The noise of the waves at dawn,
Deep blue oceans as far as the eye can see.
Exotic fish swim near the shore.
Children building sandcastles all the way down
The beach.

The sun glistens in the turquoise sky.
Seagulls stealing people's food.
The sky, cloudless and calm.
Rain, they haven't even heard of the word.

The food tastes delicious.
The smell overtakes the air.
The spices so strong they make your mouth set aflame.
The sun, the sea, the food,
In Greece!

Bradley Quinn (10)
Radclyffe Community Primary School, Salford

Football - Haiku

Wait one minute, look!
Over there, is that Gigsy?
He just scored! *Yippee!*

Man United rocks!
Rooney is the best player.
He can loop the loop!

**Carly Errington, Natasha O'Connor, Kane Davies (10)
& Shauna Cook (11)**
Radclyffe Community Primary School, Salford

I Went To Bed And Bumped My Head

I went to bed and bumped my head.
I saw a bee on TV.
I saw a fly with my eye.
I opened the door and saw the floor.
I sat on the wall and caught a ball.
I opened the shed and found my ted.

Detysha Harper (6)
Radclyffe Community Primary School, Salford

Football - Haiku

The wonderful team!
Champions League, come on now!
The crowd cheers them on!

Bliss Molyneux (10)
Radclyffe Community Primary School, Salford

A Superhero Poem

I possess an incredible power,
As I soar to the top of the Eiffel Tower.
On Monday I was doing my job well,
Until I fell into a well.
On Tuesday I was fighting crime,
I thought I was doing quite well
Until I got locked in a dark cell.
On Wednesday I was in bed,
I tried to get out then
I thought I was dead.
On Thursday a speeding bullet took over me
And hit a person that fell into the sea
That I thought I could save.
On Friday I was in hospital
Looking after the person who got hit by the bullet,
Helping him as fast as possible.
On Saturday I lost all my power
And when I tried to fly to the top of the Eiffel Tower
I got tired and fell.

Antony Marshall (10)
St Basil's Catholic Primary School, Halton

Fear - Haiku

Alone in the dark
Screaming noises around you
Frightened in the night.

Hannah Dowd (8)
St Basil's Catholic Primary School, Halton

Valentine Poem

If I were a chef
I'd cook any meal for you.
If I were a plumber
I'd clean out your loo,
But as I'm just an ordinary man,
I give you my love as best as I can.

If I were a footballer
I'd score a 46 yard free kick.
A nurse,
Not smell of sick,
But as I'm just a man in the street,
I give you my love, lay my heart at your feet.

If I were a gold miner
I'd give you my gold.
A doctor,
Cure the cold,
But as I'm only an average Joe,
I send you my love as best as I know.

Dylan Tiernan (11)
St Basil's Catholic Primary School, Halton

Mrs Douglas

Our head teacher is yellow
She is a cool summer's day
In a sunny playground
She is the sun in the air
She is a smart suit working in her office
She is a hammock swinging side to side
She is Only Fools and Horses
She is a wedding cake waiting to be eaten.

Liam Ogburn (11)
St Basil's Catholic Primary School, Halton

Valentine

If I were a swimmer
I would swim the sea for you
If I were a gold miner
I would get gold for you
But as I am just the same old man
I will give you my love as best as I can

If I were an orthodontist
I'd clean my teeth for you
If I were a train driver
I would chuff along with you
But as I am just the same old man
I will give you my love as best as I can

If I were a fisherman
I would catch fish for you
If I were a farmer
I'd plough my fields for you
But as I am just an ordinary man
I send you my love as best as I can.

Sean Franey (11)
St Basil's Catholic Primary School, Halton

A Star - Haiku

So bright in the sky
They look like little jewels
Shining all night long.

Charlotte Ducker (9)
St Basil's Catholic Primary School, Halton

The Lion Roars - Haiku

When the lion roars
The birds fly high in the sky
All are very scared.

Amy Norton (9)
St Basil's Catholic Primary School, Halton

Valentine Poem

If I were a dancer
I'd wear out my feet for you
If I were a cook
I would make delicious cakes for you
But as I'm just an ordinary man
I give you my love
As best as I can

If I were a farmer
I'd plough my fields for you
If I were a gold miner
I would give you jewels and diamonds
But as I'm only a man in the street
I give you my love
Lay my heart at your feet

If I were a singer
I'd sing my heart out for you
If I were an optician
I would see the beauty of you
But as I'm just an average man
I send you my love
As best as I can.

Rebecca Sumner (11)
St Basil's Catholic Primary School, Halton

Sticky Tar

There was a young lady called Rockstar
She stepped and fell in some tar
She said, 'Oh, yuck!
This feels like muck!'
That poor young lady called Rockstar.

Daniel Clark (9)
St Basil's Catholic Primary School, Halton

Becks Has Written A Love Poem To Posh

I would score and win for England,
Because I love you,
I would hit the ball as far as I could.

I would take a strike and hit the ball into the net,
Because I love you
And I would score the winning goal in the finals.

I would take a corner and score,
Because I love you,
I would run for the world,
Because I love you.

I would be chosen as team captain,
I would score from a mile away
And I would win the World Cup for you,
Because I love you.

Rebecca Dwyer (10)
St Basil's Catholic Primary School, Halton

Limericks

A lady from Crewe
There was a young lady from Crewe
Who suddenly started to moo
Her head started hurting
She was crazy for certain
The crazy young lady from Crewe

The young lady from Star
There was a young lady from Star
Who was really quite bizarre
She bumped her head
On a silly shed
That mad young lady from Star.

Lauren Bird (8)
St Basil's Catholic Primary School, Halton

The Builders

Rugby
Tackling, scoring,
Bleeding, hurting, fighting,
In rugby you can hurt yourself,
Chasing.

Birthday
Party, dancing,
Laughing, cheering, shouting,
People buy you presents and cards,
Surprise!

Workmen
Noisy, crazy,
Digging, sorting, driving,
They were working Thursday/Friday,
Builders.

Bradley Donovan (8)
St Basil's Catholic Primary School, Halton

Mike & Jake Limericks

There once was a man called Mike
Who liked to ride his bike
He went to the park
Until it was dark
Then went home as fast as you like

There once was a young man called Jake
Who fell in a very deep lake
He called for his friend
Who was around the bend
That's the young man called Jake.

Rebecca Littler (9)
St Basil's Catholic Primary School, Halton

Dinosaur Expert

There once was a young man from Rorator
Who was very keen on a dinosaur
He went to the show
With his teddy bear, Po
That silly young man from Rorator.

Alex Leonard (9)
St Basil's Catholic Primary School, Halton

Nightmare

Nightmare
Ghoulish, scary
Jumping, screaming, shaking
Chasing and creeping up on you
Frightened.

Siobhan Fletcher (9)
St Basil's Catholic Primary School, Halton

A Greedy Young Man From Mars

There was a young man from Mars
Who ate lots of chocolate bars
One day he popped
Everywhere had to be mopped
What a greedy young man from Mars.

Cassie Gill (9)
St Basil's Catholic Primary School, Halton

Jungle

Scary, creepy,
Eating, catching, howling,
Monkeys swinging in the high trees,
Darkness.

Demi Foley (9)
St Basil's Catholic Primary School, Halton

The Sea - The Huge Blue, Wet Bath

The sea is a blue and wet bath
And at the sun you see it laugh,
It is sky-blue on a sunny day,
Nothing is as big as it, no way.

The sea is a bath
And it is so big it can fit a shark.
You could hear it so loud,
It's like a dog's bark.

It sometimes jumps in the sky,
It gallops over the rock.
It rolls over all the time
And then hits a dock.

Elliott Hamlett (11)
St Basil's Catholic Primary School, Halton

The Lady From Crewe

There was a young lady from Crewe
She didn't know what to do
So she went to the shop
Where she bought some pop
That poor young lady from Crewe.

Lyle Coombes (9)
St Basil's Catholic Primary School, Halton

Jake

There once was a young man called Jake
Who hit himself with a rake
He didn't have much money
But he could afford to buy some honey
This young fellow called Jake.

Jon Fox (9)
St Basil's Catholic Primary School, Halton

Rat Boy's Letter

Dear Mum,
No longer am I feeling good,
Yesterday I was flying but I dropped into mud.

I thought I was the muscliest man,
But now I'm going down the pan.

I was fighting a man who I thought was jailed,
As I went to hit him, my powers failed.

I had a date with Minnie Mouse,
She let me down to watch EastEnders in her house.

My power to go back in time is not all it seems,
I've seen the beheading of two lovely queens.

Mum, I am going away for a while,
Because I am too fragile.

I went to Spain in that dreadful noisy plane,
I got lots of mozzy bites and was in loads of pain.

I don't have my long curly tail,
So no longer am I a superhero, but I deliver the mail.

I hope you're having more fun than me,
As I got stung by a big scary bee.

Your loving son,
Rat Boy.

Adam Jackson (11)
St Basil's Catholic Primary School, Halton

A Man Called John

There once was a man called John
Who went and ate a scone
He saw a bubble
And got caught in a pile of rubble
That poor old man called John.

Cameron Davie (9)
St Basil's Catholic Primary School, Halton

Jordan Has Written A Love Poem To Peter

I would hold a poisonous spider
And collect 5 challenge stars
Because I love you

I would swim in a lake of leeches
Because I love you

I would catch a python
And not wear make-up or wash my hair
Because I love you

I would take a mud bath
And climb the tallest tree in the jungle
Because I love you

I would get the birds to flap their wings and squawk
And get the crickets to chirp
Because I love you.

Alex Rathbone (11)
St Basil's Catholic Primary School, Halton

Because I Love You

I would score a goal for England
Because I love you
And strike the ball into the net

I was selected for captain
Because I love you
I would win the Premiership for you

I would try my hardest
Because I love you
And curl the ball into the back of the net

I would win the World Cup for you
Because I love you
And buy you fancy clothes

My team will win the Champions League for you
Because I love you.

Andrew McGowan (10)
St Basil's Catholic Primary School, Halton

Fire

Behold the fiery giant I am
Climbing higher and higher
Destroying everything in my path
Crackling in anger

I look to see my army at work
Burning everything in sight
I hear the crashing of wood
And screaming of people

I dance my way to the top to see my work

On Saturday I saw the building being built
And with anger I crackled and burnt it again
Then with a gust of wind, I was gone.

Jemma Hawkes (11)
St Basil's Catholic Primary School, Halton

Letter From A Failing Superhero

Dear Mum,
Things aren't going too well right now,
All I do is make *booms* or *kapows,*
It was only last week I fell off a mountain
And then I landed in a fountain!
I got stood on by Godzilla,
All because I didn't support Aston Villa!
I had a lucky escape,
When I caught my cape!
I'm always getting stuck in mud,
I hope you haven't misunderstood.
Your good-for-nothing daughter,
(Who is very close to slaughter!)
The No 1 zero hero.

Emma McKeever (10)
St Basil's Catholic Primary School, Halton

A Letter From A Failing Superhero!

Dear Mum and Dad,
I am very, very sad
On Monday, I flew into a mountain
And landed in a muddy fountain
On Tuesday, I grew too fat to fit in my suit
For the past few days I've had to eat fruit
On Wednesday, I bounced up to the ceiling
My underwear went on the outside which was revealing
On Thursday, I lost my flying power
I realised this when I flew into a tower
On Friday, I got stepped on by Godzilla
This really wasn't a thriller
On Saturday, I was eating Coco Pops
When the TV said I was wanted by the cops
On Sunday, I was blown up by a bomb
Help me, Dad! Help me, Mum!
Love, your failing hero.

Rebecca Gill (11)
St Basil's Catholic Primary School, Halton

The Sea

Behold! A gulping giant I am!
Galloping up to the sky.
I wave to the sun,
As I cover up the sand.

I look around at my army,
Kicking the rough rocks nearby.
As I see the sun disappear,
Tears fill up my eyes.

I overflow the rocks with my enormous mouth and tongue,
I see my waves washing away in the sun.
Then I realise it's night
And it's spoilt all the fun.

Lauren Maxwell (11)
St Basil's Catholic Primary School, Halton

The Sea

I lie here looking up at the sky
And I clap as I hit the rocks,
I gallop along the sand,
Raking it as I go by.

I hear the people chatting,
About the way I sprint and run,
I turn around to look at my army,
As I say goodnight to the sun.

I turn my head to look at my army,
As they follow my every move,
I give an applause to the power of the wind,
But cry as the sun starts to go.

Becky Taylor (11)
St Basil's Catholic Primary School, Halton

Whiplash Man

Dear Mum,
No longer am I feeling happy,
Each day I get wrinkly like my pappy.

The other day I went to the top of the globe,
Then I lost my flying power and shouted, 'No!'

I used to be faster than a speeding rocket,
But every time I go after it, it rips my newly-sewn pocket.

All women used to like my handsome face,
But now when they see me, they slap me into space.

I used to be able to eat a fully roasted goat,
But every time I catch and eat, I always badly choke.

It makes me feel like a failing hero,
I know I am one, because I'm zero!

Your failing son,
Whiplash Man.

Lewis Baines (11)
St Basil's Catholic Primary School, Halton

Panther

Panther
Black, very big
Pouncing, growling, running
Heavy, fierce, killing, monster
Victor.

Courtney Wilson (9)
St Basil's Catholic Primary School, Halton

The Man From Mars

There once was a man from Mars,
Who couldn't stop looking at stars,
He hit his head
On a garden shed,
That poor old man from Mars.

Tanya Holleran (9)
St Basil's Catholic Primary School, Halton

Feelings

Love is like the ocean that never runs out.
Beauty is like the swish of a silky, satin sari
That takes charge of the material of life.
Hate is like a blind bat, stuck in a horrid world.
Joy is like a tickled kangaroo, waiting to become stationary.
Sadness is like a hypnotised cat waiting to be clicked
out of punishment.
Politeness is like a homeless kitten, waiting to be found with
man-made happiness.
Rudeness is like an uncontrolled motorbike, waiting to be arrested.
Well this is the life of us, the life of us all.

Rebecca Morris-Murphy (11)
St Elizabeth's Catholic Primary School, Liverpool

When Day Becomes Night . . .

As the beaming, golden sun
Gives its last hug to the Earth,
It kisses it goodbye.
Darkness spreads and . . .
Sets the animals in a leap of panic.
As the heavens start to cry,
The grass is coated in a gleaming gloss.
The owl of death
Swoops the fields for its prey,
Its eyes like amber searchlights.
The river roars,
The land tries
To bring the fierce waves
To a halt.
A pack of wolves stare,
They whine for their mother,
All sound lost,
In the bitter, scorching winds.
As the ducks fly south,
They face the terrifyingly, blizzardly winds,
Which force them to the ground.
All of a sudden,
This natural war is over,
The sun rises
And begins to hug the Earth again.
Now night becomes day.

Josh Griffiths (11)
St Elizabeth's Catholic Primary School, Liverpool

Weather

The sun shines on the dusty wood,
The sun shines on the dark trees,
The sun shines on the filthy mud,
The sun shines on the boy's knees.

The rain pours down on the glistening glass,
The rain pours down on the colourful frame,
The rain pours down on the fresh, green grass,
The rain pours down. We know it came.

The wind blows down on the howling dog,
The wind blows down on the fluffy cat,
The wind blows down on the rolling log,
The wind blows down on the leather hat.

Now the weather has changed its way,
In this wonderful world it is no longer day.

Kayleigh Roach (11)
St Elizabeth's Catholic Primary School, Liverpool

The Whale Song

In the sea,
Swimming by me.
In the open,
Free from everything.

Not a care in the world,
Huge fins can be curled.
Splash in the sea,
Eat fish in the sea.

You don't eat like me,
You still swim in the sea.
You eat fish like me,
But you don't look or act like me.

But I still care for you,
A great mammal in the sea.

Megan Grant (10)
St Elizabeth's Catholic Primary School, Liverpool

Night

The darkness of the night
Means no more flying kites
The moon has appeared
Next it will disappear

Watch out the owl's about
Be careful it is going out
The coldness of the air
Thickens everywhere

The birds cease the song
And find their nests
The night is ending
And they need to rest

The moon is fading
The sun is rising
The night will be back
It's a matter of fact.

Amy Lahiff (11)
St Elizabeth's Catholic Primary School, Liverpool

Morning At School

Morning at school is like a boomerang,
But you are the one coming back.
Morning at school is like a burst of words
Entering your every brain cell.
Mornings at school are great
For learning new things.

Lewis Metcalf (11)
St Elizabeth's Catholic Primary School, Liverpool

My Grandma

My grandma loves reading her books,
My grandma loves watching Sky TV,
My grandma loves me showing her my pictures,
My grandma loves us visiting her,
My grandma loves eating her sweets,
My grandma loves hearing the radio,
My grandma loves sleeping,
My grandma loves playing the Lotto,
My grandma loves walking to the shops,
My grandma loves getting her pension,
My grandma loves wearing her blue velvet pants,
My grandma loves slipping into her old black shoes,
My grandma loves being around her new sofa,
My grandma loves the ocean sea,
But not as much as she loves me!

Kerry Smith (8)
St Margaret Mary's Catholic Junior School, Liverpool

The Sea

The sea is a wild horse
Tall and white, rushing about all day
Flashing its great mane
Grooming its long white body on the beautiful beach

As night falls it bows its head into the sand as it moans away
But as the next day falls, it raises its mane and plays again
As summer comes he slowly runs away into the deep dark sea

As May or June falls he will be so quiet
So quiet
He lies on the sandy banks and rocks
Slowly falling asleep
But his long mane slowly moves on the soft busy beach!

Annie Towers (8)
St Margaret Mary's Catholic Junior School, Liverpool

The Sea Is Like A Greyhound

The greyhound is rough and tough.
This greyhound leaps up out of the water!
He crashes against the rocks.
He eats the sand away.
This greyhound is vicious and very fierce!
He settles down on sunny days
And blows about on windy days!
The greyhound towers over the tiny people below.
The greyhound can be a wild beast.
It howls in the wind and he turns icy in the cold.
He settles down in June when the flowers bloom!
It is calm on the sandy beach.
When the greyhound rests on the sand, asleep.

Melissa Summers (8)
St Margaret Mary's Catholic Junior School, Liverpool

The Sea

The sea is like a mental dog,
It roars against the rocks.
The sea is like an angry dog,
When the sun goes down and the moon comes up.
The sea is like a calm puppy waiting to be fed,
It hits the rocks like a loud bark.
The waves jump like a rapid dog.
The waves spring like an excited dog.
His soaking paws are like cool and cold rocks.
When the wind roars and the moon rocks, the dog starts to sleep.
When dawn breaks, this crazy dog waggles his tail
And kills the sea.
When it is a stormy day, it improves his power.
On a sunny spring morning the sea is calm and gentle.
When the sky goes bright, it hides in its den.
When the dog gets hungry it hunts for its prey.

Chloe Duffy (9)
St Margaret Mary's Catholic Junior School, Liverpool

My Gran

My gran's hands are wrinkled and as white as snow.
My gran's face is as soft as a cuddly teddy.
My gran's eyes are as blue as the sky.
My gran's clothes are as colourful as a rainbow high in the sky.
My gran moves like a spider on ice.
My gran has memories of the olden days.
I think my gran is happy
And as cheerful as a singing bird.

Ciarán Lambert (8)
St Margaret Mary's Catholic Junior School, Liverpool

My Grandma

My grandma is round-shouldered as a question mark.
My grandma is as old as a caveman.
My grandma is as wrinkly as my grandpa.
My grandma is glued to the TV like a magnet to a fridge door.
My grandma listens to the radio all day like an animal
                                    listening for its prey.
My grandma climbs the stairs like a spider trying to get
                                    out of the bath.

David Norton (9)
St Margaret Mary's Catholic Junior School, Liverpool

The Best Gran In The World

My gran's hands are soft like a silky cushioned pillow.
My gran's face is as cute as a baby.
My gran's eyes are bluey-green like the ocean water.
My gran's clothes are baggy but still in fashion,
My gran moves like a tortoise on ice,
My gran thinks of her old memories of the olden days,
I know my gran loves me
I love my gran.

Kathleen Marmion (9)
St Margaret Mary's Catholic Junior School, Liverpool

The Sea

The sea is like a playful horse.
Crashing all day long against the rocks.
Splashing, crashing everywhere.
Can't get to sleep anywhere.
All you can hear is splish! splash! splosh!
The waves crashing, the wind blowing at the sea,
It's still like a playful horse.
The playful horse rushes about all day long.
Tall and white, sparkly fur,
Still can't get to sleep anywhere.
With clashing teeth and greasy legs,
He jumps towards the shore,
He lies along the sandy shore,
Moan, moan, all day long,
Still can't get to sleep anywhere.

John-Michael Linnell (9)
St Margaret Mary's Catholic Junior School, Liverpool

My Nan

My nan is as wrinkly as a rhino
And likes reading books.
My nan is as warm as a fire
And loves watching Sky News.
My nan is as clumsy as a clown
And as thin as a stick.
My nan is as slow as a turtle
And likes eating chocolate.
My nan is as playful as a puppy
And likes playing card games.
My nan is as cool as Kev Seed
And hates eating her tablets!
You might think my nan hasn't got time for me,
But I don't care because I know she loves me!

Antony Riley (8)
St Margaret Mary's Catholic Junior School, Liverpool

Market Poem

Come and buy!
Come and buy!
A fresh baked pie and a googly eye.

Come and buy!
Come and buy!
A game of Monopoly and some broccoli.

Come and buy!
Come and buy!
Soft cotton wool and a hairy bull.

Come and buy!
Come and buy!
Smelly fish and a dirty dish.

Come and buy! Come and buy!

Paul Jackson (8)
St Margaret Mary's Catholic Junior School, Liverpool

Market Poem

Come and buy
Come and buy
Mushy peas and smelly cheese

Come and buy
Come and buy
Worldwide maps and silver taps

Come and buy
Come and buy
Flying rockets and pants with pockets

Come and buy
Come and buy
Golden fish and a china dish

Come and buy from our market stalls.

John Doolan (8)
St Margaret Mary's Catholic Junior School, Liverpool

Come And Buy

Come and buy,
Come and buy,
Smelly cheese and squashy peas.

Come and buy,
Come and buy,
Books for finding, books for rhyming.

Come and buy,
Come and buy,
Cocktail sticks, cheese 'n' onion crisps.

Come and buy,
Come and buy,
Frilly skirts and spotty shirts.

Come and buy,
This market's the best place to go.
Come and buy.

Siobhan Smith (7)
St Margaret Mary's Catholic Junior School, Liverpool

Sounds

Bumper cars bumping
Candyfloss turning
Patties sizzling
Ketchup squirting
Food cooking
Hotdogs boiling
The noise, it keeps on going

Water guns squirting
Barbecues sizzling
Flies buzzing
People swimming
Kids shouting
Bees stinging
Yippee, it must be summer.

Mary Rossiter (8)
St Margaret Mary's Catholic Junior School, Liverpool

Market Poem

Come and buy!
Come and buy!
Juicy fruit
Lovely suits
Come and buy!
Come and buy!

Come and buy!
Come and buy!
Smart ties
Yummy pies
Come and buy!
Come and buy!

Come and buy!
Come and buy!
Lovely legs
Good pegs
Come and buy!
Come and buy!

Georgia Ashton (8)
St Margaret Mary's Catholic Junior School, Liverpool

The Zealous Zoo

The lovely lion lazily laughed at the little leopard.
The happy hippo happily hurried to the horrendous heron.
The tired tiny tigers tearfully told a terrifying tale of torture.
The mischievous monkey meanly made a massive mistake.
The cool climbing cat quietly collected cake.
The demented dozy dog drank the damson juice.
The partying pig stole pasta from the party.

Chloe Thompson (8)
St Margaret Mary's Catholic Junior School, Liverpool

Market Poem

Come and buy!
Come and buy!
Grape juice
Apple mousse
Come and buy!
Come and buy!

Come and buy!
Come and buy!
Chocolate bar
Model car
Come and buy!
Come and buy!

Come and buy!
Come and buy!
Juicy chicken
Footballs for kicking
Come and buy!
Come and buy!

Paul Ruddock (7)
St Margaret Mary's Catholic Junior School, Liverpool

Sounds

Alarms ringing,
Bottles clinking,
Radios buzzing,
Babies crying,
Cars rattling,
People shouting
Oh no! It must be morning!

Shannon Corfield (8)
St Margaret Mary's Catholic Junior School, Liverpool

Ask Jeremy Joe

If you ask a question of Jeremy Joe,
All he will say is, 'I don't know!'
Can you scare a hare with a polar bear?
Does a vampire bat have a hairy rat?
Will a hairy ape have a cape?
Will a purple shoe fit a kangaroo?
Can a tiger cup go to a pub?
Will a chimpanzee kiss me?
You can keep asking Jeremy Joe
But all he says is, 'I don't know!'

Amelia Gregory (7)
St Margaret Mary's Catholic Junior School, Liverpool

Anger

Anger is red like a fierce flame of fire,
Anger smells like smoke coming out of my ears,
Anger tastes like hot curry,
Anger sounds like a car skidding round the corner,
Anger feels like getting whacked on the head,
Anger reminds me of when I don't get what I want!

Mark Gurrell (8)
St Margaret Mary's Catholic Junior School, Liverpool

Sounds

Alarms ringing,
Bottles clinking,
Radios buzzing,
Dogs barking,
Children crying,
Engines roaring,
Oh no, it must be morning!

Jessica Lewis (7)
St Margaret Mary's Catholic Junior School, Liverpool

The Sun

As calm as a beautiful flower
Waiting in the garden for the rain to come

As lively as a puppy playing in the hard
Rough mud

As creepy as a lion getting ready to
Jump at you

As hot as a fire coming towards you

As shiny as a gold medal round your neck

As unexplored as a newborn chick popping
Its head in and out of its shell

As blazing as a shooting star racing through the air

As disturbing as a loud dog
Howling through the night

As sparkling as the Queen's crown placed
Carefully on her head

As strong as the air floating in the sky.

Molly Unsworth (9)
St Margaret Mary's Catholic Junior School, Liverpool

Anger

Anger is red like hot tomatoes on the stove.
Anger smells like a candle burning quickly.
Anger sounds like people shouting in a crowded room.
Anger feels like red-hot flames burning in the night.
Anger reminds me of when my brother took my PlayStation
                                        games from me.

Laura Manning (8)
St Margaret Mary's Catholic Junior School, Liverpool

My Best Friend

My best friend is Ian,
He makes me laugh
When he tells me funny jokes.
My best friend is Ian, everyone,
He is kind and friendly
And plays basketball with me.
My best friend is Ian,
He makes me happy.

Jordan Tynan (7)
St Margaret Mary's Catholic Junior School, Liverpool

Anger

Anger is pure red like a squashed tomato in a boiling cauldron.
Anger smells like red gas in a can ready to burst.
Anger sounds like steam blowing out of your ears with loud music.
Anger feels like a bumper car hitting you in the back.
Anger reminds me of when I wanted to go to bed at 10 o'clock
                              and my mum said, 'No!'

Emily Cornwall
St Margaret Mary's Catholic Junior School, Liverpool

The Exotic Garden

I strolled through the garden
And I smelt the scent of a soft sunflower
I saw a shimmering , sparkling crystal-blue fountain
I could taste sweet, lovely, tasty strawberries
I heard the sound of a bluebird singing
And the grass, curving in and out of my toes.

Jessica Rimmer (9)
St Margaret Mary's Catholic Junior School, Liverpool

My Gran

My gran is a hundred years old.
She shops at Netto.
My gran is very tired all the time,
She often sits down and goes to sleep in her rocking chair.
My gran looks after her husband well.
He is very lazy, so my gran turns the telly off
And shouts at him to get out of bed.
My gran gives me a fiver
And says, 'Give me a love.'

Jack Currie (9)
St Margaret Mary's Catholic Junior School, Liverpool

My Squirrel

My squirrel is a smart fellow,
He will always sniff and smell,
He has the bushiest tail
And my squirrel is so cute.

My squirrel loves his nuts,
He will collect and run away,
I don't like to stay for long, I am worried,
Be nice, I will stay for a while.

My squirrel is a cheeky fellow,
He will rob nuts from his friends,
Then run up a tree and hide,
Then go on the look-out.

My squirrel is red and fuzzy,
He won't need a coat in winter,
Even though he hibernates,
That means that he is lucky.

Chloé Manning (8)
St Margaret Mary's Catholic Junior School, Liverpool

My Morning Poem

This must be morning because
The sun is shining
I hear birds tweeting
My mum opens my curtains
The sun shines on me
Mum goes downstairs for breakfast
Then my alarm clock is ringing
And I'm waking
I'm yawning
I'm dressing
I look through the window
I see leaves moving
I hear car horns beeping
I hear cars stopping
While I'm brushing my teeth
Then I wash my face
So this must be morning.

Kodee Peers (8)
St Margaret Mary's Catholic Junior School, Liverpool

My Gran

My gran loves being outside in the garden
She relaxes but she doesn't like cats
When she sees a cat, she quickly goes inside
And closes the door
My gran bought an angry dog
For scaring the cat away
The dog hasn't caught the cat yet!

Shahnam Kazforoosh (9)
St Margaret Mary's Catholic Junior School, Liverpool

The Sea

The sea is a roaring, terrifying lion
Rushing down past me like a cheetah
It is like a growling bear
That's making waves with its paws
At night the tide comes in like a bat
In the day the sea is like a polar bear's soft fur
In the evening the sea is like a cat and harmless
In the night the sea crushes the rocks like a rhinoceros.

Adam Jackson (9)
St Margaret Mary's Catholic Junior School, Liverpool

Market Poem

Come and buy!
Come and buy!
Sponge cakes
Quality rakes
Come and buy!
Come and buy!

Come and buy!
Come and buy!
Cricket bats
Beautiful hats
Come and buy!
Come and buy!

Come and buy!
Come and buy!
Juicy meats
Special treats
Come and buy!
Come and buy!

Oliver Stone (8)
St Margaret Mary's Catholic Junior School, Liverpool

A Wounded And Useless Soldier

Bombs taking off, planes roaring across the sky
People hiding, fire everywhere, boots muddy
And bullets shooting powerfully, people screaming and dying.

Bullets screaming, bombs gliding into the woods
People crying for their mums and dads
Rain dripping into my boots
Air slimy, muddy, drop, drip, drop

I'm away from my family, I feel sad
I need to hide in the trenches
I can feel the wind coming to knock me over

I can dream of this war ending
I need to go home, I'm wounded
My friends are dead
I wish this fighting would stop!
Countries versus countries, it's so bad

When will this war end?
I want to go home
I can't now, *uh*, I'm dead!

John Connor (8)
St Margaret Mary's Catholic Junior School, Liverpool

Little Miss Muffet

(Based on nursery rhyme 'Little Miss Muffet')

Little Miss Muffet
Sat on a tuffet
Eating her fish and chips
Along came a tiger
Who walked up beside her
And said, 'Are you hungry today?'

Hannah Ryan (8)
St Margaret Mary's Catholic Junior School, Liverpool

A Soldier In The War

I can see burning fires, flames getting darker,
People screaming, people in pain.
Guns shooting, blood dripping, people hiding.

I can hear bombs crashing against the floor,
People crying in pain, swords crashing.

I can feel cold rain lashing down on my head and my neck,
Feel tired and fed up.

I dream of being at home, seeing my kids
And giving them a kiss before they go to bed.

I hope for the war to stop
And be safe at home.

Sarah Von Bargen (7)
St Margaret Mary's Catholic Junior School, Liverpool

The Haunted House

Two skeletons hanging on the wall
Four ghosts playing basketball
Six vampires having a nap
Eight mummies rapping a rap
Ten Frankensteins doing a tap dance
Twelve bats wearing pink pants
Fourteen pumpkins being cooked
Sixteen trembling children being spooked

Aagghh! What a scary place to be!

Katelyn Webb (8)
St Margaret Mary's Catholic Junior School, Liverpool

Grandad

My grandad is as kind as God,
My grandad gives me nine pounds every week.
I love my grandad very, very much.
My grandad smokes, but I still love him
And Grandad loves me too.
He comes to my house every week.
He is never nasty and he never shouts.
I could not wish for a better grandad.

Georgia Hampson (9)
St Margaret Mary's Catholic Junior School, Liverpool

My Grandpa

My grandpa is the best grandpa in the world
He's warmer than the sun
He's even the best in the west
He's the champion of the world
But best of all he's super Grandpa.

Robert Crowney (9)
St Margaret Mary's Catholic Junior School, Liverpool

The Sea

The sea is like a shark
It is splashing its tail
Making a noise in the sea
Sharpening its teeth on living things
Waiting for people to come
So the shark can eat them
The sea is crystal like the shark's colour
The waves are like its fins
Moving up and down
The shark is blue like the sea
Camouflage flashing in the water.

Luke Hughes (9)
St Margaret Mary's Catholic Junior School, Liverpool

When I Grow Up

When I grow up, what will I be?
A superstar singing in concerts.
A superstar - that's what I'll be.

When I grow up, what will I be?
A fisherman catching loads of silvery fish.
A fisherman - that's what I'll be.

When I grow up, what will I be?
A gymnast leaping and twirling.
A gymnast - that's what I'll be.

When I grow up, what will I be?
A chocolate maker making yummy chocolates.
A chocolate maker - that's what I'll be.

When I grow up, what will I be?
A golfer winning every trophy there is.
A golfer - that's what I'll be.

But for now I'm a schoolgirl working all day.

Amie Calvert (8)
St Margaret Mary's Catholic Junior School, Liverpool

The Sea

The sea is like a roaring, terrifying, angry lion
Rushing down fast like a cheetah
It is like a growling bear making waves with its paws
At night the tide comes in like a bat
In the day the sea is like a polar bear's fur
In the evening the sea can be like a soft cat that's harmful
In the night the sea crushes the rocks.

Matthew Murphy (9)
St Margaret Mary's Catholic Junior School, Liverpool

A Teacher In The Staffroom

Different teachers all around me,
Children calling and shouting and teachers chatting to me,
A cup of tea with sugar in my hand,
I dream of spending some time with my lovely family!
I hope for a lovely, jubbly, comfortable lie-in in a glamorous bed.

Faye Flynn (8)
St Margaret Mary's Catholic Junior School, Liverpool

Shy

Shy is yellow like the soft sand,
Shy smells like a blooming flower,
Shy tastes like cold ice cream.
Shy sounds like love,
Shy feels like a friendly hug,
Shy reminds me of being safe.

Sophie Mannion (8)
St Margaret Mary's Catholic Junior School, Liverpool

Little Miss Flynn

(Based on nursery rhyme 'Little Miss Muffet)

Little Miss Flynn sat on a tin
Eating her chocolate cake
Along came a tiger
Who crept up behind her
And scared Miss Flynn away
Miss Flynn thought she had no skin
And the tiger said, 'Oh splendid'
And mended the chocolate cake
They danced all night
Never had one fright
And married at the end of the day
And they both said, 'Wahay!'

Erin Lonergan (7)
St Margaret Mary's Catholic Junior School, Liverpool

My Morning Poem

This must be morning because
I wake up and start yawning,
Hear birds singing,
Mum gives me a calling,
The trees are swaying,
Children laughing and playing,
Teeth brushing,
Out to school I'm going,
So, this must be morning.

Holly Shipley (7)
St Margaret Mary's Catholic Junior School, Liverpool

Fairground Sounds

Dodgems crashing
Race cars skidding
People laughing
People shouting
People winning
Come on, let's go home.

Daniel Sutherland (8)
St Margaret Mary's Catholic Junior School, Liverpool

My Soft Auntie Ann

My soft Auntie Ann
Has a cake whenever she can.
She sits on the sofa watching TV.
My soft Auntie Ann likes to have a cuddle with me.
She gives me jelly babies - soft and sweet
And helps keep our writing lovely and neat.
That's my soft Auntie Ann.

Emily Sutherland (8)
St Margaret Mary's Catholic Junior School, Liverpool

Come And Buy

Come and buy,
Come and buy,
Fish and chips
And a sweety mix.
Purple grapes,
Candy capes,
Walking sticks,
A clock that ticks.
A uniform,
A bag of corn,
Get some peas
And seeds for trees.
Pots and pans,
Metal cans,
Shimmery fish,
A Chinese dish.
A rubber band,
A fake sticky hand,
Some pixie dust,
A piece of crust.
A pair of nails,
A packet of snails,
Some tasty fruit,
A golden flute.
Let's go away,
To eat and play.

Bethany Fearon (8)
St Margaret Mary's Catholic Junior School, Liverpool

The Sun

The sun is a red ball flying through the sky.
The sun is a giant firework setting off in the sky.
The sun is a yellow bouncy ball jumping up and down.
The sun is an orange sandpit getting hotter every minute.

Jessica Dooley (9)
St Margaret Mary's Catholic Junior School, Liverpool

Shy

Shyness is pale blue like rushing waterfalls.
Shyness smells like a fresh field of corn.
Shyness tastes like a red rosy apple.
Shyness sounds like a soft sweet voice.
Shyness feels like a feathered bushy quilt.
Shyness reminds me of when my friends spread my secret.

Emily Hignett (8)
St Margaret Mary's Catholic Junior School, Liverpool

Love

Love is red like a popped heart.
Love smells like a fresh bed of roses.
Love tastes like a hot cup of tea.
Love sounds like two birds singing a sweet song.
Love feels like a kiss on the lips.
Love reminds me of a special date.

Kate Wilson (8)
St Margaret Mary's Catholic Junior School, Liverpool

Embarrassment

Embarrassment is pink like a squashed peach.
Embarrassment smells like roses in a living room.
Embarrassment sounds like a song on the TV.
Embarrassment feels like my face is squashed.
Embarrassment reminds me of the infants in my first class
When I went to talk to the teacher.

Morgan Challinor
St Margaret Mary's Catholic Junior School, Liverpool

Kindness

Kindness is sunshine shining in your face.
Kindness smells like the blossom in the springtime.
Kindness feels like helping someone when they can't find their friends.
Kindness sounds like the birds singing in the leafy trees.
Kindness reminds me of when someone was sitting on their own
and I asked them to play with me.

Alex Laidaw (7)
St Margaret Mary's Catholic Junior School, Liverpool

A Footballer On A Football Pitch

I can see flying balls, a big huge goal with a ball in it,
I can hear the crowd singing, the ball getting kicked,
I can feel the ball getting to my head,
I dream of getting in the Champions League,
I hope for my team to win.

Joseph Robinson (7)
St Margaret Mary's Catholic Junior School, Liverpool

Horse Riding

Horse riding is fun, like running in the sun.
Horse riding is funny, like a bunny.
The horse gallops all day, like it is flying all day.
Horse riding is good, like running in the mud.
Horse riding is like jumping over the sun.
Horse riding is as great as it can be.
Horse riding is great like jumping over the gate.

Gabrielle Flude (8)
St Margaret Mary's Catholic Junior School, Liverpool

Excited

Excited is yellow when you feel happy and you're looking straight up.
Excited smells like lovely red roses.
Excited sounds like lots of people shouting and screaming
When my football team scores a goal.
Excited feels like you're very nervous but happy all at the same time.

Ellie Clarke (7)
St Margaret Mary's Catholic Junior School, Liverpool

Morning Sounds

Birds singing,
Brothers shouting,
Sausages sizzling,
Dads snoring,
Balls bouncing,
Sun shining,
Wind whistling,
Hammer hammering,
Knee hurting,
Trees swaying,
Bees buzzing,
Lemonade popping,
Toast burning,
Kettle bubbling,
People praying,
Cats miaowing,
Dogs woofing,
Wolves howling,
Cars hooting,
Wheels skidding,
Phone ringing,
Music roaring,
Taps splashing,
Oh no, it's morning!

Lia McHale (8)
St Margaret Mary's Catholic Junior School, Liverpool

A Soldier In World War II

I can see bombs exploding,
Cannons firing,
Soldiers hiding,
Buildings falling,
Families dying.

I can hear children crying,
Machine guns cracking,
Tanks crashing.

I can feel the ground shaking,
Hearts banging,
Anger burning.

I dream of winning the war,
Going home.
I hope for the war to end.

Ryan Cowell (8)
St Margaret Mary's Catholic Junior School, Liverpool

Jeremy Joe

If you ask a question of Jeremy Joe
All he will say is, 'I don't know!'

Can you go to the fair with a polar bear?
Does a vampire bat eat a hairy cat?

Will a hairy ape wear a grey cape?
Can you go to the loo with a kangaroo?

Can a tiger cub go to the football club?
Will a chimpanzee go to sea?

You can keep on asking Jeremy Joe
But all he will say is, 'I don't know!'

Olivia Hussey (7)
St Margaret Mary's Catholic Junior School, Liverpool

Pet Shop Poem

There's a pet shop on our block,
Whoever goes there gets a shock.
Kangaroos being kickers,
Pesky snakes stealing stickers.
Rattlesnakes shaking their charms,
Silly iguanas pushing alarms.
Licking lizards being named,
While loud lions are being tamed.
A hamster with an injured knee,
Lazy chameleons watching TV,
Tiny ants trying on pants,
Smelly rats and scary bats.
Cheeky monkeys continuing to chatter,
Laughing hyenas cracking jokes,
Thirsty frogs drinking cokes.
Noisy parrots eating carrots,
Tiny mice nibbling cheeses,
Silly snakes full of sneezes.
Flipping flamingos playing with nets,
No one ever bought those pets.

Joseph McLean (8)
St Margaret Mary's Catholic Junior School, Liverpool

My Gran

My gran is warm like a fluffy bear,
She's like hot chocolate on a cold winter's evening.
My gran is the hot sun in the summer
And the comfy soft bed I sleep on at bedtime.
My gran is the moon and stars in the night sky.
My gran is the whole world!
My gran is everything to me.

Megan Jones (7)
St Margaret Mary's Catholic Junior School, Liverpool

Anger

Anger is red like boiling hot and bubbling tomato sauce on the stove.
Anger smells like sweating, after people running.
Anger sounds like the Devil shouting really nasty things very loudly.
Anger feels like speeding roller coasters crashing into me.
Anger reminds me of not getting an ice cream from the ice cream man.

Aiden Hoffman (8)
St Margaret Mary's Catholic Junior School, Liverpool

Market Poem

Come and buy!
Come and buy!
Chocolate mousse
Lovely juice
Come and buy!
Come and buy!

Come and buy!
Come and buy!
Pigs' feet
Lovely meat
Come and buy!
Come and buy!

Come and buy!
Come and buy!
Sugar lumps
Squashy flumps
Come and buy!
Come and buy!

Joseph Rimmer (7)
St Margaret Mary's Catholic Junior School, Liverpool

Grandma And Grandpa

My grandma is wrinkly,
Sometimes her eyes are twinkly,
Her whole body is crinkly,
What shall we do about it?
My grandpa drives me round the bend,
Like a car zooming past,
Sometimes we have to amend,
To become friends.
My grandpa talks about World War II,
Sometimes we don't know what to do!
Sometimes it's quite boring,
Will he ever stop snoring?
My grandma loves smoking,
Sometimes she starts choking,
She never stops joking,
When she's smoking.
My grandma and grandpa are so funny,
They like to call me Honey.

Elizabeth Anderson (9)
St Margaret Mary's Catholic Junior School, Liverpool

Sounds

Alarms ringing
Birds tweeting
Taps dripping
Bottles clinking
Radios buzzing
Doors banging
Oh no, it must be morning.

Abigail Wright (7)
St Margaret Mary's Catholic Junior School, Liverpool

Megan's Special Shopping List

What shall I buy?
I'll buy a kite
To fly high in the sky
I'll buy a stripy top
With a floppy mop and fizzy pop
To drink when I'm dry

What shall I buy?
I'll buy cuddly toys and
Tasty McCoys
Smelly socks
And grey soft rocks

What shall I buy?
I'll buy a wooden frame
And a cool game!
A strawberry pie
And a hairy fly
Then I'll say *goodbye!*

Megan Brady (8)
St Margaret Mary's Catholic Junior School, Liverpool

Embarrassment

Embarrassment is pink like someone's cheeks
when they go on stage.
Embarrassment smells like air freshener and polish
after my mum has cleaned.
Embarrassment sounds like a band called, 'The Killers'.
Embarrassment feels like squashing yourself together
and wanting to hide.
Embarrassment reminds me of kissing my dad
in front of my friends.

Chelsea Arnold
St Margaret Mary's Catholic Junior School, Liverpool

The Zoo

In my zoo there is . . .

One orange octopus
Swishing through the huge water tank.

Two terrifying tarantulas
Scaring all the animals away.

Three turquoise tortoises
Getting slower and slower.

Four fine frogs
Hopping like mad.

Five fantastic fancy fish
Dancing around the fish pond.

Six strange sheep
Barking instead of bleating.

Seven stupid snakes
Always bumping into everything.

Eight entertaining elephants
Doing lots of extravagant shows.

Nine naughty newts
Getting into lots of mischief!

Ten tall tigers
Roaring and ro-ar-ing - *grrr!*

What a crazy place to visit for the day!

Lorna McMahon (8)
St Margaret Mary's Catholic Junior School, Liverpool

When I Am Older

What will I be when I'm older?
I know . . .
I'll be a bike rider
Going up and down on the ramps
A bike rider - that's what I'll be.

Or shall I be a bungee jumper?
Bouncing around - *boing - boing!*
A bungee jumper - that's what I'll be.

Shall I be a footballer
Scoring goals?
Yes, a footballer - that's what I'll be.

When I am older, what shall I be?
A zookeeper
Looking after the pink flamingos,
A zookeeper - that's that I'll be.

But for now, I'll just be me!

Liam Vance (8)
St Margaret Mary's Catholic Junior School, Liverpool

My Grandad

My grandad is as soft as a cushion.
My grandad is as funny as a clown.
My grandad is in a band.
My grandad is as cool as an ice cube.
My grandad is as nice as a sweet.
My grandad is as cute as a kitten.
My grandad is the best.

Jessica Costigan (9)
St Margaret Mary's Catholic Junior School, Liverpool

Worrying

Worrying is black like a shaking washing machine.
Worrying smells like off cheese in a bread bin.
Worrying sounds like the Titanic song.
Worrying feels like a dry and sore throat.
Worrying reminds me of going to the museum and art gallery.

Chloe Russell (8)
St Margaret Mary's Catholic Junior School, Liverpool

Happy

Happy is bright red like a big smile.
Happy smells like an air freshener in a posh living room.
Happy sounds like a cheerful and blissful voice.
Happy feels like I want to burst out with laughter.
Happy reminds me of when I scored my first goal for my team.

Aaron Manley (8)
St Margaret Mary's Catholic Junior School, Liverpool

Come And Buy

Come and buy
Come and buy
A stinky fish and a shiny disk
Come and buy
Come and buy
Some pyjamas and a packet of bananas.

Ceiran Hall (8)
St Margaret Mary's Catholic Junior School, Liverpool

Ask Jeremy Joe

Could you eat a pear with a polar bear?
Does a vampire bat need a hairy hat?

Will a hairy ape eat a massive grape?
Can a kangaroo talk to you?

Can a tiger cub eat a tub?
Will a chimpanzee chop my knee?

Joseph Fitzpatrick (8)
St Margaret Mary's Catholic Junior School, Liverpool

The Candle

As the candle burns orange, yellow and bright,
The flame flickers strong and powerful,
Moving back and forth, shining, glowing.

The candle flame, a sign of hope,
Breaking through the darkness,
Remembering the lost.

Daniel Grayson (9)
St Mary's CE Primary School, Manchester

I Love My Mum

I love my mum, she's the best in town,
I love my mum, she wears a funny frown.

I love my mum, she has a magical smile,
I love my mum because you can see her smile from a mile.

I love my mum, she's the happiest there can be,
I love my mum because she loves me.

Olivia Lee (9)
St Mary's CE Primary School, Manchester

Fairies

Friendly fairies grant your wildest wish
Friendly fairies eat off a silver dish

Evil fairies meddle about
Evil fairies make you scream and shout

Friendly fairies twirl around in a ring
Friendly fairies love to dance and sing

In the day, evil fairies have a sleep
But at night they try to make you weep

Friendly fairies have beautiful wings
Friendly fairies can do magical things

Evil fairies make you sleep for one hundred years
Evil fairies prey on your greatest fears.

Taylor Shaw (10)
St Mary's CE Primary School, Manchester

Goldfish Acrostic

G is for a gliding fish
O is for orange, silver, gold and blue stones
L is for their long orange tails
D is for darting across the tank
F is for fish food
I is for ice-cold water
S is for swimming quickly
H is for holidays, when we go on holiday
   we give them a special food, which breaks down
   over a period of days.

Emma Tommins (9)
St Mary's CE Primary School, Manchester

My Groovy Granny

I have a groovy granny
I guarantee she's not like yours
She never makes me cook or clean
Or do any other chores

I have a groovy granny
Oh, she's just the best
She never knits me sweaters
Or multicoloured vests

I have a groovy granny
She wears mini skirts and jeans
She even plays football with me
And she's always on my team

I have a groovy granny
She wears earrings to the floor
And when she goes out shopping
She just has to buy some more

I have a groovy granny
She uses wrinkle cream and dye
She doesn't like her natural hair
Hmm, I wonder why?

I have a groovy granny
She's always on the go
But ask me, 'Would you swap her?'
And you'll get a great big *'No!'*

Vanessa Beckles (10)
St Mary's CE Primary School, Manchester

My Hamster

As I sit here in my cage,
The wheel I'm on is all the rage,
Please take me out so we can snuggle,
I promise you I will not struggle.

It's okay, I will not bite,
As long as you don't give me a fright.
If you put me in my ball,
You can still see me - I'm not that small.

But don't forget to feed me,
Because you really, really need me.
Will you drop me? Never, never,
You and me, we'll be friends forever.

Katie Butler (9)
St Mary's CE Primary School, Manchester

My Pet Budgie

Oh my budgie, he's so very sweet,
you should hear him chirp and tweet.
His name is Tweety, he's green and yellow,
oh, what a handsome little fellow.
He has a lovely beak that is beige,
which he uses to open his cage.
He likes to make a lot of noise,
especially when he plays with his toys.
His favourite food is sunflower seeds,
you should know that because that's what he needs.
He loves to fly around the room,
the problem is I have to go round with a broom.
I think my budgie is the best,
although sometimes he can be a . . .
Pest!

Katie Pollit (9)
St Mary's CE Primary School, Manchester

Under The Sea

The sea is blue, the starfish are orange
The shells are cream
And the sharks are mean.

The seaweed is green and
The mermaids are a dream,
With their long shiny tails
And their golden veils.

The male whale hails his mate
And sings, 'Come on darling, we'll be late.'
The shark swims by
With a glint in his eye.

He sees the swordfish as bait
And in his hunger he just can't wait,
Lashing and gnashing, he takes a swipe
And gives the old swordfish a great, big fright.

When the shark took a great, big bite
The sea horse joined into the fight
And told the shark,
'This isn't right.'
Then they rowed throughout the night.

All the other creatures thought what a sight
To see the sea horse and the shark fight
Then they both saw the light
And bid each other a very good night.

Freya Holmes
St Mary's CE Primary School, Manchester

Red

Red is like a rose, with a strawberry smell
Red is like a cherry, juicy and ready to be eaten
Red is like a strawberry, juicy and refreshing
Red is like blood, dripping and dropping
Red is my favourite colour.

Lucy Haslingden (10)
St Michael's CE Primary School, Manchester

My Annoying Little Brother

My annoying little brother
Is as smelly as a pig,
He has a bald head,
But he likes to wear a wig.

He eats like a horse,
He's as tall as a giraffe,
His feet are as long as a metre stick
And he has a weird laugh.

He is very, very dumb
Because he has no brain,
He thinks he's so clever,
But I think that's insane.

Sadly my annoying little brother
Will always be family,
So I will have to accept it
And that's how it will forever be.

Heather Gofton (10)
St Michael's CE Primary School, Manchester

At The Circus

The weird funny clown
Stripped right down
Then he fell off the stage
And it was a rage
I enjoyed that day
That day in May.

Bethany Trevor (10)
St Michael's CE Primary School, Manchester

Blue

Blue is the colour of the sky
Where birds and planes fly.

Blue is the colour of the sea
Which crashes against me.

Blue is the colour of the water
Which splashes on my clothes.

Blue is the colour of the rain
Where little drops go down the drain.

Blue is the colour of the painting
Which is nice and glittering.

Blue is my favourite colour ever!

Kirstie Luu (10)
St Michael's CE Primary School, Manchester

Desert Island

My ship has sunk,
Just my luck.
I'd only been sailing four days,
'Cause of my daring ways.
There's nothing to eat,
So I'm really sleepy.
There's nothing to drink,
I can't properly think.
I feel drowsy,
As well as lousy.
I'm stuck in Hell - *help!*

Shannon Brady (10)
St Michael's CE Primary School, Manchester

On The Plane

I'm on the plane
Going to Spain
There isn't much noise
Just kids playing with toys
There is a movie
It's not very groovy
A man's sleeping
The plane's beeping
Drinks are coming
The guy next to me is humming
I don't like the food
It's put me in a mood
We're about to land
I can see the sand!

Cian Bates (10)
St Michael's CE Primary School, Manchester

The Writer Of This Poem

(Based on 'The Writer of this Poem' by Roger McGough)

The writer of this poem
Is richer than a king
As clever as a teacher
And was born in spring

As strong as an ox
As wise as an owl
As cheeky as a monkey
As bossy as Simon Cowell

The writer of this poem
Walks in different ways
He trips and flips and slips
(Or so the poem says!)

Thomas Butterworth (10)
St Michael's CE Primary School, Manchester

You Can't Deny The Style

You can't deny the style of a tile,
You can put them in a pile and sort them in a file,
You can't make them smile and put them on trial,
But you can certainly use them for a shopping aisle.

Rhys Nuttall (10)
St Michael's CE Primary School, Manchester

Finding Things

If you've lost your ruler, shoe or your pen,
You know you will soon see them again.
If you've lost your toy, your phone or your car,
You just know they've not gone far.
If you've lost your chair, bag or a book,
You will always get them if you look!

Ben Lee (10)
St Michael's CE Primary School, Manchester

The Camera

I had a stupid little camera
It didn't have a flash
I dropped it on the floor once
It shattered with a crash

The next day I tried to fix it
I tried to no avail
I got so annoyed with it
I sold it in a sale.

Marcus Rowe (10)
St Michael's CE Primary School, Manchester

Blue

Blue is like rain
coming down quickly.

Blue is like the sea
crashing and bashing.

Blue is like a whale
huge and large.

Blue is like the sky
wonderful and calm.

Blue is the colour of my bedroom
bright and dark.

Blue is like my flowers
making the garden peaceful and relaxing.

Blue is like stone
sparkly and fantastic.

Blue is an amazing colour.

Blair Bowles (9)
St Michael's CE Primary School, Manchester

My Little Brother

My little brother,
If he does not get his own way,
He will scream and shout all day,
We will try to make him laugh
And we will try to calm him down,
But whatever we do, he will still sound an alarm!

Emily Oliver (10)
St Michael's CE Primary School, Manchester

One Autumn Day

First comes the leaves
Falling from the trees
Then comes the frost
Covering all the moss
The empty branches sway in the wind
Making all the litter fly out of the bin
This is a real autumn day!

Meghan Dunham (10)
St Michael's CE Primary School, Manchester

The Writer Of This Poem

(Based on 'The Writer Of This Poem' by Roger McGough)

The writer of this poem
Is taller than can be
As keen as mustard
Stronger than my knee

As fast as a cheetah
As smart as a cat
As sharp as a pen nib
As blind as a bat

(So the poem says!)

Nathan Stringer (9)
St Michael's CE Primary School, Manchester

Anger!

Anger is red like my football that I named Fred,
It tastes like fire in my throat,
Anger is tall, not short at all,
Anger is pain, just like you're in the rain,
But anger is all I am.

Eben Rayworth (9)
St Michael's CE Primary School, Manchester

Holiday

I hear the sea coming in and out, *splash and crash*
I look up to the sky, the sparkling turquoise glistening in the sun
I touch the sand, it's glowing in my hands

I see sea creatures crawling and swimming, carefully and cautiously
I look behind the horizon, a dark blue, quiet and calm

I feel that this holiday should not come to an end
I will miss you.

Charlotte Earnshaw (10)
St Michael's CE Primary School, Manchester

The Writer Of This Poem

(Based on 'The Writer of this Poem' by Roger McGough)

The writer of this poem
Is richer than chocolate
Loves to go to Florida
On the rock 'n' roller coaster

Going up and down
On the tower of terror
She has a friend
Who went away forever

(So the poem says!)

Abigail Greatrex (9)
St Michael's CE Primary School, Manchester

Anger

Anger is the colour of red.
Anger is like fire in my eyes.
Anger makes people jealous and upset.
Anger is pain,
Falling down like rain.
I hate anger!

Catherine Wright (9)
St Michael's CE Primary School, Manchester

Skilfully Played

Skilfully, swiftly lobbed the ball
Dribbles quickly through the players
Had a shot and triumphantly scored
Running wildly with arms waving.

Joel Carrigan (10)
St Michael's CE Primary School, Manchester

The Football Match

Cheering fans
Beer to drink
Score it
Save it
Arguing fans
All ninety minutes
Pass! Pass!
The whistle blown
For the end of the match
What an exciting game!

Iain Bird (10)
St Michael's CE Primary School, Manchester

Football

A child scored a goal
A boy fell down a hole
All you could hear was cheering
But one girl had bad hearing
The boy was running down the pitch
And then he saw an ugly witch
Arrrggghhh!

Michael Butt (10)
St Michael's CE Primary School, Manchester

Flowers

Flowers are pretty,
Flowers are fragrant,
Flowers are bright,
Flowers are light,
Flowers are shiny,
Flowers are tiny.

Dean Feather (10)
St Michael's CE Primary School, Manchester

Happiness

Happiness is bright orange like a shining sun,
Sounds joyful like a tune in my heart
And tastes like buttery Italian tagliatelle.
It smells of rich chocolate delight,
It's lovely to look at, like the stars from a fairy's wand.
Happiness is going shopping for clothes.
Happiness reminds me of my mum.

Francesca Lidgley (10)
Victoria Hosptial Paediatric School, Blackpool

Sadness

Sadness sounds like raindrops clashing on a living room window,
It tastes like Mexican spices running down my throat.

Sadness smells like bad carrots,
Sadness looks like someone's crying a river of tears.

Sadness feels like cold custard running through my soft gentle hands,
Sadness reminds me of someone's funeral you love very much,
Knowing you'll never see them again.

Jessica Campbell (10)
Wilson's Endowed CE Primary School, Carnforth

Happiness

Happiness sounds like a robin tweeting in the cold winter snow,
It sounds like a happy man whistling loudly and high-pitched,
Walking down the street,
A sweet juicy chicken fillet tastes like happiness,
Happiness tastes like a soft, juicy tomato,
A bunch of daffodils opening in the morning sun smells
like happiness,
Happiness looks bright and colourful,
A warm breeze blowing at me feels like happiness,
Happiness feels like a soft squashy teddy bear,
Happiness is like a shining yellow,
A beaming orange is like happiness,
Happiness reminds me of a group of people laughing.

Joshua Forrest (10)
Wilson's Endowed CE Primary School, Carnforth

Animals

Hyenas laughing at the lions,
Elephants squirting water around,
Turtles plodding slowly and carefully,
Mice squealing so quietly,
Snakes slithering and sliding up and down,
Newts hiding as people approach,
Alligators snapping their large jaws,
Lions roaring as they catch their prey,
Rats scattering for food,
Dogs barking as they chase cats,
Leopards sat in trees being lazy,
Cheetahs running like a supersonic car,
Tigers having lunch with zebras,
Owls searching like searchlights for mice,
Cubs playing and running round and around,
Whales eating plankton as they go round,
Hedgehogs sticking their spikes out as they hide.

Shannon McGuire (10)
Wilson's Endowed CE Primary School, Carnforth

The Lion

The lions basking in the shade of the acacia tree.

Strong and majestic, the lion brings down a large zebra,
Stunning and golden-furred, she drags it to her prowling pride,
They accept it gracefully and tear it limb from limb,
While she waits in the shade of the acacia.

The lions basking in the shade of the acacia tree.

The lion leaps upon a log,
I can hear a drum in the distance, is that what disturbed her?
A cub's miaowing call draws her away,
She runs to where it lies, its tawny fur a mess
And smoothes it down, until he sleeps.

The lions basking in the shade of the acacia tree.

A Masai tribe run past, still the lions sleep,
Their shining fur is ruffled by the African wind,
Then they stir,
The lions wake to a sudden chill,
Their stomachs rumbling.

The lions basking in the shade of the acacia tree.

The lions leap upon a passing gazelle,
Suffocating it,
But as they eat,
The cub is alone,
Until a poacher carries him off.

The lions basking in the shade of the acacia tree,
But . . .

There's one less lion now.

Amber Perryman (11)
Wilson's Endowed CE Primary School, Carnforth

Love

Love sounds like a mother singing a lullaby to her child.
Love sounds like the calm beating of waves on the shore.
Love tastes of luscious honey.
Love tastes of sugar, fine and sweet.
It smells like jasmine flowers.
Love smells like a bride's bouquet,
As she walks down the aisle.
Love looks like the diamonds of moonlight
Twinkling on a lake.
It looks like an emerald carpet of endless sea,
Foaming and splashing.
It feels like the silky rose petals
And the softness of marshmallow clouds.
Love's colour is a bright, bubbly pink.
It reminds me of a kiss on the cheek,
It reminds me of when Dreamland encloses me to sleep.

Anna Galbraith (9)
Wilson's Endowed CE Primary School, Carnforth

Flowers In The Summer

I can see large locus flowers blooming in the sun,
Golden daffodils, they might blind you if you look,
Red poppies popping in the fields
And the cherry-red tulips, just like scolding teacups.
Grasshoppers hopping to and fro,
Brightly coloured butterflies fluttering nearby,
Six spotted ladybirds flap their tiny wings to try
And get to another plant.
As I feel the nettles they sting my thumb,
Luckily there is a dock leaf nearby,
Yellow sunflowers so big and so bright,
The stem is so rough,
Petals of a lavender plant fall into my palm.

Georgia Mackenzie (9)
Wilson's Endowed CE Primary School, Carnforth

Happiness

Happiness sounds like the laugh of a hyena,
It also sounds like the chirping of a bird in an oak tree,
A blackbird singing sounds like happiness,
Happiness tastes like a lovely juicy apple freshly picked,
It tastes also like the fresh countryside,
The sweets from the sweet shop taste like happiness.
Happiness smells like freshly cooked bacon,
It smells like a handful of bright red roses,
A happiness smell is a hot Sunday dinner.
Happiness looks like a little toddler playing in the sun,
It also looks like sparrows perching on the old oak tree,
A little baby playing on the ground looks like happiness.
Happiness feels like soft pink candyfloss,
A blossom tree blowing in the wind feels like happiness
And happiness feels like a flat football on a hot day.
Happiness is the colour red, it reminds me of a hot day,
Happiness reminds me of my first Christmas.

Megan Greenwood (9)
Wilson's Endowed CE Primary School, Carnforth

The Big Race!

I can see the Ferrari Enzos zooming into the distance,
With its wheels spinning supersonically,
Sun beaming down on the metallic Mclaren F1,
While exhausts blast out fire and brake pads burn.

I can hear the racing revs of the fearsome fast Ferrari,
Applying new brakes, struggling to halt,
Tyres turn through puddles
Making the water cascade upwards,
Nearby crowds vociferating their views.

I can feel the wind gushing in my face
As the golden yellow Lamborghini Murgelago dashes past,
As if the Ferraris and Mclaren F1s were going too fast.

Daniel Robinson (10)
Wilson's Endowed CE Primary School, Carnforth

Red Squirrels

Bushy red tails and tufty ears concludes the arrival of red squirrels.
The sound of little clawed feet jumping from tree to tree
Is the noise of the agile red rodent.
I hear a crack and look up, a small juvenile, auburn,
Woodland creature penetrates the brittle outer shell of a pine cone.

The squirrel scans the woodland canopy
Searching for Scot's pine cones,
The tiny mammal soars through the needle
Like leaves off the tree.
Her ears erect, she looks around, she knows danger is near.
For under her perch is a dark pine-marten waiting to attack.

The rodent runs, clawed feet pattering on the pine's noisy bark,
Out of the gloom she is being secretly spied upon
As the cat-shaped figure is hungry
And then the pine-marten attacks,
He chases the young squirrel through the branches,
But far in the distance there is a shot,
Both predator and prey freeze in their tracks.
The pine-marten draws back to his gloomy shelter

And for now the squirrel is safe.

Jack Hobbs (11)
Wilson's Endowed CE Primary School, Carnforth

The Sea

I can see mussels tightly closed never to be revealed,
Seagulls swirling above the water waiting to plunge into the sea,
Seaweed trying to haul itself out of the sand,
Cranky crabs craving for food,
Fishes swimming slowly along the shore,
There's never going to be a key to open up the ocean door.

I can hear children laughing loudly whilst they are
                              playing beach tennis,
Waves crashing over and over, one after another,
Seagulls squealing and squawking noisily,
Water smoothing rough rocks,
Fishes swimming slowly along the shore,
There's never going to be a key to open up the ocean door.

I can feel the coldness of the water on my feet,
Seaweed swirling softly around my sandals,
Happy because it is a beautiful day,
Crumbling sand crawling into my flip-flops,
Fishes swimming slowly along the shore,
There's never going to be a key to open up the ocean door.

Rebeka Thomas (10)
Wilson's Endowed CE Primary School, Carnforth

Happiness

Happiness tastes like a freshly picked strawberry,
Happiness tastes like pizza margarita,
Happiness tastes like slippy eggs in a frying pan.

Happiness, happiness feels great.

Happiness smells like a freshly cut rhododendron,
Happiness smells like a chocolate ice cream,
Happiness smells like a glass of fresh orange.

Happiness, happiness feels great.

Happiness reminds me of a toddler chasing a Jack Russell.

Happiness, happiness is great.

Louise Plowden (11)
Wilson's Endowed CE Primary School, Carnforth

Animals

I can see birds flying,
Dogs running around,
The sky jumping and leaping,
Rabbits bouncing around,
Guinea pigs eating strawberries
And cleaning their faces,
I can hear dogs barking,
Birds singing,
Cats purring,
Cats miaowing,
I feel happy when I stroke the guinea pig,
I feel happy when the birds sing,
I feel joyful when I rub the soft cat.

Karla Fraser (11)
Wilson's Endowed CE Primary School, Carnforth

The Cat

I see the cat crouching with its white velvet paws on
                                luscious green grass,
Long, fluffy tail waving high in the clean air,
Large, wide, blue eyes scanning the surrounds,
Ginger fur blowing in the breeze.

I hear the cat swishing its golden, gleaming tail in glorious glamour,
A soft gentle purr fills the air,
Amongst the quiet pit-pat of paws,
Loud panting is ever present.

I feel the cat's warmth radiating off her golden fur,
A small head butts against my hand,
A purr echoes in the long grass,
It sends out hot breath.

I know the cat.

Alec Escolme (11)
Wilson's Endowed CE Primary School, Carnforth

Happiness

Happiness sounds like laughing and bright red, ruby robins
Singing in the blossom of the trees,
It tastes like a bacon sandwich and a cup of tea in bed,
Happiness smells like roast beef and mash on a Sunday lunchtime,
It looks like an Old English puppy rolling around,
Buried in long green grass which comes up to your knees!
Happiness feels like playing on your trampoline,
Trying to get to the sky!
Its colour is bright orange like a juicy fruit,
It reminds me of my family playing cricket on a Saturday night,
When the sun is setting and the smell of burgers
                                cooking on the barbecue.

Molly Thomas (10)
Wilson's Endowed CE Primary School, Carnforth

Happiness

Happiness sounds like a tweeting bird,
It sounds like a group of giggling girls.
Happiness tastes like a sweet cylinder of sherbet,
A bowl of warm, melted milk chocolate tastes like happiness.
Happiness smells like a loaf of freshly baked bread,
A pink rose in full bloom smells like happiness.
Happiness looks like a young girl skipping on a lawn of green grass.
A small child snug in their bed looks like happiness.
Happiness feels like a pure, white, fluffy cloud,
It feels warm in the fresh air.
Happiness is yellow like a banana from the fruit bowl.
Happiness reminds me of a group of people,
Laughing with the sun blazing down.
My friends remind me of happiness.

Janet Wightman (11)
Wilson's Endowed CE Primary School, Carnforth

Camping

Cars *splash, splash*
Owls *hoot, hoot*
Bats *flap, flap*
Sleeping bags *rustle, rustle*
The little drips and flows
People going up and down the stony path
Where they go, no one knows
Children talk, giggle and laugh
Cars *splash, splash*
Bats *flap, flap*
Sleeping bags *rustle, rustle.*

Kenya Hardie (8)
Wilson's Endowed CE Primary School, Carnforth

Animals

I can see a fluffy, tired hamster eating some food,
A slippery, scaly snake sliding along,
As a cat is waiting to be fed
And a dirty, rough elephant spraying water.

I can hear a hamster nibbling at his cage,
Cats purring as they're getting stroked,
Dogs barking as people pass.

I can feel a fluffy, soft hamster,
A slippery, scaly snake,
A rough, dirty elephant
And a smooth wet whale!

Scott McLachlan   (10)
Wilson's Endowed CE Primary School, Carnforth

The Pub

Glasses *cling, cling*
Pool balls *clack, clack*
Men go *glug, glug*
Pop goes *slurp, slurp*
Up and down the crowded bar
Talk, bang, roar and *screech*
People leave in their cars
Talk, bang, roar and *screech*
Glasses *cling, cling*
Pool balls *clack, clack*
Men go *glug, glug*
Pop goes *slurp, slurp.*

Andrew Taylor   (8)
Wilson's Endowed CE Primary School, Carnforth

The Sound Of Animals

Dogs bark, bark
Cats miaow, miaow
Tigers roar, roar
Monkeys oo, oo
The cows in the field give a little moo
Ferrets scratch in their boxes
Horses crunch apples in the field
Ferrets scratch in their boxes
Dogs bark, bark
Cats miaow, miaow
Tigers roar, roar
Monkeys oo, oo.

Zara Johnston (8)
Wilson's Endowed CE Primary School, Carnforth

Christmas

Reindeers *clip, clop.*
Bells *tingle, tingle.*
Santa's boots *creak, creak.*
Rooftops *bang, bang.*
A red nose sways *whoosh, whoosh.*
Through the snow travelling
Back to the North Pole,
Santa shouts, 'Ho, ho, ho!'
Travelling back to the North Pole.
Reindeers *clip, clop.*
Bells *tingle, tingle.*
Santa's boots *creak, creak.*
Rooftops *bang, bang.*

Sarah Galbraith (8)
Wilson's Endowed CE Primary School, Carnforth

The Sounds In School

Children *whisper, whisper*
Chairs *screech, screech*
Bottoms *wiggle, wiggle*
Teachers *shout, shout*

All the children doing their work
Pens and pencils *screech* and *scratch*
Teachers reading sums and more
Pens and pencils *screech* and *scratch*

Children *whisper, whisper*
Chairs *screech, screech*
Bottoms *wiggle, wiggle*
Teachers *shout, shout.*

Ryan McLachlan (8)
Wilson's Endowed CE Primary School, Carnforth

Knights

Breaking lances *crack, crack!*
Horses' hooves *stamp, stamp!*
Sharp swords shining, shining!
Large shields *thrack, thrack!*

Tournament starts with a roaring crowd.
Breaking lances all around.
Fighting knights to their death.
Battling dragons' fiery breath.

Breaking lances *crack, crack!*
Horses' hooves *stamp, stamp!*
Sharp swords shining, shining!
Large shields *thrack, thrack!*

Peter Holmes (9)
Wilson's Endowed CE Primary School, Carnforth

The Noisy Zoo

Monkeys *oo, oo*
Zebras *neigh, neigh*
Seals *ee, ee*
Giraffes *chomp, chomp*
Zookeepers getting food ready
Washing out water bowls
A little seal finds a teddy
It has fallen into its bowl
Monkeys *oo, oo*
Zebras *neigh, neigh*
Seals *ee, ee*
Giraffes *chomp, chomp.*

Katy Stevenson (7)
Wilson's Endowed CE Primary School, Carnforth

The Jungle Poem

Monkeys *swing, swing*
Lions *roar, roar*
Snakes *hiss, hiss*
Giraffes *crunch, crunch*

In the jungle there are snakes, giraffes
Lions and lots of animals
Rain starts pouring
Like snakes, giraffes, lions and lots of animals

Monkeys *swing, swing*
Lions *roar, roar*
Snakes *hiss, hiss*
Giraffes *crunch, crunch.*

Evan Forbes-Anderson (7)
Wilson's Endowed CE Primary School, Carnforth

Winter Days

Winter days *snow, snow*
Turkey *chip, chip*
Presents rattle, rattle
Puppies *woof, woof*
Children sleeping in the middle of the night
When Father Christmas is coming to your house
Winter days *snow, snow*
Turkey *chip, chip*
Presents *rattle, rattle*
Puppies *woof, woof.*

Emma Woodend (7)
Wilson's Endowed CE Primary School, Carnforth

The Planet Cheese

Rockets *rumble, rumble*
Cheese *tumble, tumble*
Alien eggs *crumble, crumble*
Echoes *mumble, mumble.*

Aeroplanes zoom through the sky
Aliens always passing by
Clouds fading in the sky
Aliens always passing by.

Rockets *rumble, rumble*
Cheese *tumble, tumble*
Alien eggs *crumble, crumble*
Echoes *mumble, mumble.*

Sally Wightman (9)
Wilson's Endowed CE Primary School, Carnforth

The Arcade

Car games *zoom, zoom*
Pool balls *clack, clack*
Dance mats *boom, boom*
Penny games *ching, ching*
Little children on horse games
Starting to come first place
Little children on horse games
Laughter, laughter all the way
Car games *zoom, zoom*
Pool balls *clack, clack*
Dance mats *boom, boom*
Penny games *ching, ching.*

Nile Wood (9)
Wilson's Endowed CE Primary School, Carnforth

In The Classroom

Children *whisper, whisper*
Teachers *screech, screech*
Pens *scrape, scrape*
Chairs *screech, screech*

In the classroom the teacher screeches
Children start to whisper
Teacher shouts, bellows and screeches
Children start to whisper

Children *whisper, whisper*
Teachers *screech, screech*
Pens *scrape, scrape*
Chairs *screech, screech.*

Molly Warburton (9)
Wilson's Endowed CE Primary School, Carnforth

My Garden

Tree house *creak, creak,*
Birds' wings *swish, swish,*
My cat *peek, peek,*
Wind blows *whoosh, whoosh.*

Hiding in the tree house,
While watching birds fly past.
I see not a single mouse,
While watching birds fly past.

Tree house *creek, creek,*
Birds' wings *swish, swish,*
My cat *peek, peek,*
Wind blows *whoos, whoosh.*

Madeleine Hobbs (9)
Wilson's Endowed CE Primary School, Carnforth

Farms

Digger *screech, screech*
Trailers *bang, bang*
Sheep dogs *bark, bark*
Tractor *roar, roar*
The quadbike zooms past
Farmer slams barn door
Hometime at last
Work has finished
Digger *screech, screech*
Trailers *bang, bang*
Sheep dogs *bark, bark*
Trailers *roar, roar.*

Joshua Spedding (9)
Wilson's Endowed CE Primary School, Carnforth

Quarries

Quarry sirens *whistle, whistle*
Crushers *screech, screech*
Boulders *bang, bang*

The grinding of the stones
The shouting of the men
The bell rings, time for home
Sounds just like Big Ben

Quarry sirens *whistle, whistle*
Crushers *screech, screech*
Boulders *bang, bang*
The grinding of the stones.

Aaron Ward (9)
Wilson's Endowed CE Primary School, Carnforth

Quarries

Dust *puff, puff*
The explosives go *bang, bang*
The shut door goes *screech, screech*
The rocks in the lorries go *crash, crash*

The lorries rolling on the road
Thunder, rumble, roar and *screech*
Lorries being washed, water flung everywhere
Thunder, rumble, roar and *screech*

Dust *puff, puff*
The explosives go *bang, bang*
The shut door goes *screech, screech*
The rocks in the lorries go *crash, crash.*

James Fletcher (9)
Wilson's Endowed CE Primary School, Carnforth